INTRODUCTORY PSYCHOLOGY SERIES

SOCIAL PSYCHOLOGY

By Tony Malim and Ann Birch

ISSN 0953-1564   ISBN : 1-871010-01-2

Published by Intertext Limited
Equity & Law Building
30-34 Baldwin Street, Bristol, BS1 1NR

Cartoons by Sally Artz
Designed and Produced by Colourways, Clevedon, Bristol

CONTENTS

ABOUT THE AUTHORS

Tony Malim has a first degree from Cambridge in classics and history and a Masters Degree in Education with specialization in psychology from Lancaster University. He has taught A level psychology virtually from its inception as a pilot project in 1972 and has been an assistant examiner in the subject.

Ann Birch has a Masters Degree in Education with specialization in psychology from Bristol University and is a member of the British Psychological Society. She has taught psychology at A and A/O levels for seven years and currently lectures psychology and teacher education at Weston-super-Mare College of Further Education and is a visiting lecturer at Bristol Polytecnic. She is an assistant examiner of O/A level psychology.

INTRODUCTION

This is the second in our new series of introductory texts for Advanced Level Psychology. While these books are aimed primarily at those who are studying the syllabus for the AEB A level examination we hope they will be just as useful for those who are aiming at other syllabus' - JMB A level or perhaps GCSE. Indeed, they may well prove valuable for those who are studying Psychology for the first time in Higher Education. Our aim has been to provide a set of comprehensive notes as a basis for further study and reading. Accordingly they may be used as an introduction to an area of work, to supplement work done in class, as a set of revision notes, or as an aid for those who are doing most of their study on their own. With these people particularly in mind we have provided a set of objectives at the start of each chapter to give you an idea of what you might be expected to know at the end of it as well as self assessment questions at the end of each section.

It is recommended that you take one section at a time, read carefully and then attempt to answer the self assessment questions. You should then have a good basis on which to found your further reading - either from those sources indicated at the end of each chapter or elsewhere.

This second volume deals with social psychology. Besides A level students, it will also prove suitable for those on BTEC Business and Caring Courses, and at first degree level. It includes relevant theory, up to date research evidence as well as some practical applications of social psychology. The contents include material on the following areas :

Impression formation and person perception

Attraction and liking

Attitudes - formation measurement and change

Prejudice

Norm formation

Compliance conformity and social influence

Small groups

Leadership

Pro and anti-social behaviour

We very much hope you will enjoy it.

Tony Malim
Ann Birch

"THE HECK WITH 'REALISM' — NEXT
TIME I'M OPTING FOR 'MANIPULATION'!"

Chapter 1

Introduction and Methods

At the end of this chapter you should be able to

1   Describe the main aims of social psychology.

2   Identify the problems that exist in striking the balance between 'realism' and 'rigour'.

3   Show an understanding of the problems frequently thrown up by the researcher's choice of subjects.

4   Highlight possible ethical problems that might arise from the methods of investigation adopted.

5   Identify the relationship that exists between the development of theory and the collection of data.

What is it about?

Social psychology is about people's social behaviour. When they come into contact with each other they behave in a consistent way, and there is a pattern in the way they form attitudes to people, objects and events. It is these consistencies that social psychologists try to explain and so to predict people's future behaviour.

Methods in social psychology

The problems with which a social psychologist is faced consist of striking a balance between 'realism' on the one hand and 'rigour' on the other. Do they act as 'flies on the wall' and simply observe and analyse how people behave to each other and in each other's company? If so, it is hard to generalise from what is observed at the moment and to attempt to provide causes for the effects that are observed. Or do they deliberately set out to manipulate events, set up situations in which subjects as actors will perform their roles. The more tightly controlled the situations that are designed, the more remote they become from the reality of what happens 'out there'. Of particular relevance here are the subjects that researchers choose for these carefully controlled 'laboratory experiments'. In many instances they have been captive groups of university students chosen for little other reason than that they happened to be around and available and often glad to accept the fee which researchers have sometimes used to encourage them to participate. These are of course not typical samples of the population and it is known that volunteers behave untypically. Orne suggests that they exhibit **'demand characteristics'** - they are anxious to behave in the way they believe the researchers who have taken them on want them to behave. **(Orne 1962)**

Frequently researchers have used the strategy of employing stooges to provide a particular social context in which the subjects are obliged to act without being aware that these 'stooges' are not genuinely free and independent individuals. An example of this might be the investigations that Asch conducted into conformity to social norms. In these experiments **(Asch 1956)** - reported fully in Chapter 4 - stooges of the experimenter reported seeing lines as similar in length to a test line when they manifestly were not, in order to set up a situation where subjects might conform to these erroneously created majority norms. In some cases - as with Milgram's investigations into obedience, again reported in full in Chapter 4 - subjects then discovered that they had behaved in a way of which they would never have considered themselves capable in more ordinary circumstances. There remains the question of whether it is ethically right to put individuals into this position. An alternative to this deception is 'role-playing' and this is sometimes used, as in **Jones' (1961)** investigation of attribution - quoted in Chapter 2 - where a tape recorded interview situation was used of actors role-playing alternative conditions. But is it possible for someone acting out a role to become so involved that they really do behave in the way that a person naturally would in the given circumstances?

Theory and investigation

In order to have a reason for investigating a particular piece of behaviour it is necessary to have arrived at a theory - that is a framework of ideas about the topic under discussion, which will provide a basis for the collection of data. Otherwise the data collected and the measurements made, may have a random character. However the theory itself has an influence upon the data that is collected and there is always the possibility that only that data is collected which is likely to support the theory. In this book we shall highlight the theories which have been developed in each area and make some attempt to point up the limitations of the research which tests these theories. It is important that any conclusions drawn are tentative ones. There is no proof in social psychology, only ideas which receive more or less support.

Self Assessment Questions

1   What are the main aims of social psychology?

2   Describe and make some evaluation of alternative approaches to investigating social psychological problems.

3   What ethical and other problems are thrown up by the choice of subjects and the design of studies in social psychology?

4   What is the relationship between the theories and the investigations of those theories in social psychology?

Further Reading :

Henri Tajfel and Colin Fraser (eds.), 1978, **Introducing Social Psychology,** Harmondsworth Penguin Books, Ch. 1.

"THEY'RE PERFECTLY HARMLESS — I'VE
LOCKED THE HOUSE AND THE GARAGE,
AND NOTIFIED THE LOCAL POLICE."

Chapter 2

The Perception of Others

At the end of this chapter you should be able to :

1   Show some of the ways in which we sift and select those features to which we pay attention when making judgements about a person's character.

2   Describe what is meant by **'implicit personality theory'** and some of the ways in which we may arrive at an assessment of an individual's implicit personality theory.

3   Identify what is meant by the **attribution process** in the judgement of a person's character.

4   Describe such factors as **'intention', 'norms' and 'social cues'** in the context of the attribution process and show what part they each play.

5   Describe **Kelley's model** for the attribution process and make some judgement as to its usefulness.

6   Show how errors may occur in the process of attribution.

7   Identify some factors which may cause us to be attracted to another person.

8   Describe what is meant by the **'ingratiation' effect and the 'extra credit'** effect.

9   Show how sociograms may be used to identify patterns of attraction and influence in a group.

10   Describe the main components of prejudice.

11   Show how prejudice may be the result of specific traits of personality in an individual.

12   Evaluate some theories of the origins of prejudice - eg. scapegoat theory, exploitation theory, socio-cultural, personal and social factors.

When we meet or come into contact with other individuals, we tend to make judgements about them on the basis of cues provided by them, coupled with evidence from our own experience of meeting people. In this chapter we shall look at some of the ways in which this perception of others has been studied and the factors which seem to influence our judgements. We shall also look at the factors that tend to prejudice us against some people and cause us to be attracted to others

SECTION I

STEREOTYPING AND IMPLICIT PERSONALITY

Schneider Hastorf and Ellsworth (1979) have identified six processes which they see as being involved in person perception :

1 **Attention :** this is the input stage. The items we may pay attention to include physical appearance, the context in which behaviour occurs, and the behaviour itself. We then select certain features and categorise them according to our previous experience.

2 **Snap Judgements :** we may make a direct inference from a person's appearance or his/her behaviour which does not require much cognitive effort. It may be an immediate feeling about a person - either attraction or repulsion - or else a stereotyped judgement. We might, in other words, be picking out a feature of a person's appearance or behaviour and then using it to make a total judgement about that person.

3 **Attribution :** this is dealt with fully in the second section of this chapter and involves inferring personality or attitude from observed behaviour.

4 **Trait Implication :** the knowledge that a person may possess a trait may imply to us as perceivers that he or she may well possess other traits. We have implicit theories about the way traits occur together in individuals. This may involve stereotyping or what is known as 'implicit personality' theory or perhaps the 'halo' effect, ie. a good looking girl may be assumed also to be intelligent and good- natured.

5 **Impression Formation :** an individual may be thought to possess a cluster of personality traits such as sincerity, modesty, seriousness, etc. This provides a global impression of that person. His/her characteristics are organised in our minds so that they form a coherent impression?

6 **Prediction of Future Behaviour :** we need to be able to predict how a person is likely to behave in the future, and so we use the characteristics we perceive of that person and organise these in our minds to help us to predict their behaviour.

Implicit personality theory

We tend, as a result of our experience of people, to form theories as to how personality is organised and structured. We may have a theory that a person, who is obsessively tidy in his/her habits, will also be punctilious about timekeeping, very careful about money and will give a lot of thought to decisions before acting on them. We have no evidence in the case of a particular individual that it is true, but it gives us a basis, albeit a fairly wobbly one, for making predictions about future behaviour. Various techniques have been used in psychology to uncover this **'implicit personality'**.

1 Trait Inference Method : Subjects may be told that a person has a particular attribute - say dominance - and are then asked to rate the likelihood that he or she will have other attributes such as extraversion or conservatism. It is then possible, taking a large number of subjects, to see the extent to which the attributes occur together and so to predict, given any one of these attributes, the extent to which the other attributes are associated with it. The problem with this method is that it is the experimenter who chooses the trait names and these will probably not be the ones which the subject would have used spontaneously. Are these genuine traits of personality that you are studying, or simply the words which are applied to personality traits?

2 Correlation of Traits : Subjects may be asked to rate people they know on a number of personality traits and then each trait is correlated with every other trait to provide a basis for an implicit theory of personality, that is to say, evidence for which traits go together in people's minds. **Rosenberg and Jones (1972),** for instance, used the novels of Theodore Dreisen as the basis for a study of implicit personality. They listed all the words and terms used in the descriptions of his fictional characters, and computed the number of times each occurred together in the description of a character. This provided a basis for the analysis of the implicit personality theory of Theodore Dreisen. It appeared to have two dimensions :

a) **The sex of the character.** Males and females have different personalities.

b) **Conformity to norms.** There seemed to be two types of people, one successful and conforming, the other free and unconventional.

The problem with this and similar studies again is that it is concerned with words rather than with the concepts that lie behind the words.

✗ **3 Kelly's Repertory Grid Technique (Kelly 1955) :** This technique involves asking subjects to write down the names of people who occupy particular roles - mother, boss, friend, colleague, etc. Then to ask, having grouped these people in every possible combination of three, how two were alike, and the third was different. The ways in which the subject saw them as alike were referred to as 'constructs'. The ways he/she saw the third as different were 'contrasts'. Linkages between constructs were then examined and the subject's implicit theories of personality uncovered.

4 Stereotyping : Stereotyping is closely linked to the idea of implicit personality. A single item of information about a person may generate inferences about other aspects of his/her behaviour or personality. This may be limited to some external feature - appearance, ethnic origin, occupation, for example. From this very limited information judgements are generated as to what the person is like. Good looking individuals are likely to be rated more highly on other desirable characteristics, such as intelligence, emotional adjustment, poise or kindness

Individual stereotypes

This can mean the inferring of a wide range of personality traits from very marginal evidence such as a name, physical appearance, attractiveness, etc.

Harari and McDavid (1973) showed that name stereotypes were associated with particular characteristics. David, Michael, Karen and Lisa were favourable and Elmer, Hubert, Bertha and Adelle were unfavourable. This was shown to result in a significantly higher grading of essays produced for teachers by the favourably as opposed to the unfavourably named children.

Dion et al (1972) found that photos of attractive people in photographs were credited with more desirable qualities.

Group stereotypes

This implies the application of traits to an individual once they are shown to belong to a particular group (eg. Turk, German, Jew, homosexual). **Allport (1954)** claims that stereotypes do contain a grain of truth. The evidence for group stereotyping includes a study by **Karr (1975/8)** where homosexuals were shown to be more tense, shallow, yielding, passive and quiet than men labelled as heterosexual.

In a study reported by **Karlins, Coffman & Walters (1969)** stereotypes of groups of under-graduates from Princeton University were examined to see how they had changed between 1933 and 1967. Researchers provided their subjects with lists of ethnic groups - Americans, Italians, Jews, Germans, Irish and Blacks - together with lists of words describing personality traits. They were asked to apply the personality traits they thought appropriate to each ethnic group. A comparison was then made between lists applied in 1933 and in 1967 by similar groups of students. Figure 1 opposite shows how stereotypes seem to have faded over three generations of students :

Figure 1

Americans	1933	1967	Italians	1933	1967
Industrious	48	23	Artistic	53	30
Intelligent	47	20	Impulsive	44	28
Materialistic	33	67	Musical	32	9
Progressive	27	17	Imaginative	30	7
			Revengeful	17	0

Jews	1933	1967	Germans	1933	1967
Shrewd	79		Scientific	78	47
Mercenary	49		Stolid	44	9
Grasping	34		Methodical	31	21
Intelligent	29		Efficient	16	46

Irish	1933	1967	Blacks	1933	1967
Pugnacious	45	13	Superstitious	84	13
Witty	38	7	Lazy	75	26
Honest	32	17	Ignorant	38	11
Nationalistic	21	41	Religious	24	8

'On the fading of social stereotypes in three generations of college students'. M. Karlins, T.L. Coffman & G. Walters (1969) from Journal of Personality and Social Psychology, 1969, 13:1 1-16.

Criticism : It is possible to criticise the methodology employed in this study on several scores :

1 The subjects were given the list of characteristics and so were to an extent 'fed' with possible characteristics rather than being allowed a free choice.

2 You might argue that the results do not so much illustrate changes in stereotypes over three generations as changes in the nature of the culture in which they lived.

3 The figures above represent the percentage of subjects who applied these labels to particular groups. One subject's concept of say

'religious' or 'ignorant' might be quite different from another's and, almost certainly, there would be general differences over three generations.

4   What is being studied in many cases is not the judgements that people make on the basis of their personal experience meeting Turks or Jews or Germans, but hearsay about these groups of people.

Other studies of stereotyping include that of **Bruner Schapiro and Taguiri (1958).** In this study subjects were given a trait - 'intelligence' for example - and asked whether those who were intelligent

very often are   ]
tend to be   ]   aggressive, awkward, active, etc.
may or may not be   ]
tend not to be   ]

A list of 59 traits was given to subjects who were asked to use two or three traits in combination. There was substantial agreement on those traits that were grouped together. Again we have the problem that we are dealing with trait names rather than the traits themselves.

Self assessment questions

1   What were the processes which Schneider Hastorf and Ellsworth identified as being involved in **Person Perception?**
2   What is meant by **Implicit Personality Theory?**
3   What techniques have been used to discover a person's implicit personality theory? Do they appear to be effective?
4   In particular, describe Kelly's **Repertory Grid Technique** and make a judgement on its validity.
5   What evidence has been found for the existence of **stereotyping** in people's perception of personality?

SECTION II

ATTRIBUTION

We make observations all the time of the verbal and non-verbal behaviour of those we meet, and use these observations to make inferences about what they are like.

We use terms like **'disposition', 'character'** or **'personality'** to describe the more enduring features of people and to summarise the behaviour we have observed and the judgements we have made. We are also able to predict from these observations that, in appropriate circumstances, this kind of behaviour will recur.

Attribution process

Attribution is the term used to describe the way in which we make judgements about people's feelings, attitudes and dispositions from their verbal and non-verbal behaviour. First, we locate the cause of the behaviour - the term used for this is **'locus of cause'** - as being either inside the 'actor' or within his/her environment. For example, if a person lurched up to a display cabinet and knocked a piece of china off it, we might imagine that he intended to smash the china **(an internal locus of cause** which might imply that he had a temper). But if we knew that he had tripped over a rug and put his hand out to save himself, the cause of his behaviour is seen to be outside him **(external locus of cause). Heider (1958)** called this process the **Attribution Process. Jones and Davis (1965)** explored the causes of behaviour and their implications for judgements of personality and identified three factors which tend to be involved.

1 Intention : There is a distinction made between behaviour which is intended and that which is caused by circumstances outside the individual. Also, an assessment has to be made of the individual's 'power to act'. For example, when we observe someone performing a task and want to make a judgement about his/her intelligence, we need also to take into account how difficult the task is.

2 Norms : It is necessary also to match behaviour against 'established norms of behaviour', ie. what most people would do in the same circumstances. For example, if most people get nine out of ten mathematical problems right the person who only got two right would be judged to be stupid. The more the behaviour we observe deviates from the norm, the more confidence we are likely to have in attributing enduring characteristics to the 'actor'.

3 Social Cues : A politician is expected to appear grave and sincere. That is what is expected of him/her and so is little indication of what his/her personality really is An actress is under great social pressure to appear vivacious, so that vivacious behaviour does not reveal much of her real character.

We have a good idea of what people do in a given set of circumstances. If they do this it does not tell us much about them. It is only when behaviour deviates from this that we can infer what they are really like.

Study by Jones (1961)

Tape recordings were played to subjects of job interviews, with an appli-

11

cant and a personnel officer. Subjects were told what characteristics the job required. Subjects had to assess the interviewees' characters, and say how much confidence they put in their judgements under two conditions

1 Where subjects heard candidates describe themselves in terms highly congruent with the job requirements, ie. they described themselves in a way which matched what was required.

2 Where subjects heard candidates describe themselves incongruently with the requirements of the job, ie. their descriptions of themselves did not match what was required.

Far greater confidence was placed in judgements made under the second condition. However, realism would suggest that it was unlikely that anyone up for a job would describe himself in terms totally at odds with the requirements he was aware were those of the job. This tends to be a problem with role play: the actors cannot easily get so fully into the part they are playing as to be really convincing.

Kelley's Model (1967)

Kelley saw three factors as influencing attribution of personality characteristics from behaviour.

1 **Distinctiveness :** If Hilda always wears a green dress when Harry comes to dinner and never otherwise, it could be said that she wears it because Harry is there. Her behaviour has a distinctive 'locus of cause'.

2 **Consistency :** If a person always runs away from barking dogs whenever he meets them this might indicate that he/she is a timid kind of person, afraid of dogs. The **locus of cause** is **internal,** it says something about his character. If, however, he runs away from one particular barking dog on one particular occasion, this is maybe a particularly ferocious dog. It tells us little about him, but just about a particular set of circumstances.

3 **Consensus :** When a person behaves in a particular way it is necessary to consider whether everyone behaves in this way, or whether he is the only one. If he is alone in behaving in the way he does, this fact reveals something of his character (it implies an **internal locus** of cause). If, on the other hand, everyone behaves like this, then the **locus of cause** is **external.** We have learnt no more about his character, but just what everyone does.

A test of Kelley's model was carried out by McArthur (1972). Subjects were presented with a number of statements describing the reaction of a particular person to a particular stimulus (eg. John laughs at a comedian). These statements were accompanied by three other statements which indicated consensus, distinctiveness and consistency. For each set of information, the subjects were asked to state whether it was probable the person's response was due to

12

1   Something about the person
2   Something about the circumstances
3   Something about the stimulus
4   Some combination of factors

An example might be :
*   A person you know arrives at a formal dinner party in jeans
    and an open-necked sports shirt.
Additional information about this person includes the following statements

1   "Old Harry never dresses up for any occasion"

This would indicate **"consistency"** in Harry's behaviour.

2   "Old Harry makes a point of not dressing up whenever Charles throws
    a party"

This statement would suggest that Harry normally dresses to suit the occasion except when Charles is giving the party. This "non- dressing" has an element of "distinctiveness" which says more about Harry's relationship with Charles than about Harry's character.

3   "Old Harry knows that Charles' dinner parties are always easy-going
    affairs"

This indicates an element of **"Consensus"**. Everybody knows that Charles' parties are never really formal even when they are billed as such.

As Kelley's model had predicted, subjects stated that the response had been due to something about the person himself most frequently in cases of **low consensus, high consistency** and **distinctiveness.**

Errors of Attribution : In some cases information on consensus, distinctiveness and consistency is not easy to obtain. In such cases observers have to rely on what are known as **'causal schemata'** - ie. some kind of theory about what the three sources of information would have been if they could have got hold of them.

Nisbett and Ross (1980) showed that one of the most usual errors was to assume that information was more representative of an actor's repertoire than it actually was. Extreme effects seem to be related to extreme causes. If a person suddenly packs up and emigrates to Australia we attribute this to extreme causes. We would infer trouble with the law, or disappointment in love, rather than him/her having just read a very attractive brochure from the local travel agent. If we find that there is no such extreme cause we infer that he/she is 'impulsive', perhaps, - **an internal 'locus of cause'.** Where an 'actor' behaves in an unexpected or

13

unusual way, we are motivated to look for causes and particularly internal ones. Our expectations of individiduals are derived from

1   **The group of which he/she is a member :** eg. someone may expect black children to perform poorly in schools and so an unexpectedly good performance leads him/her to infer high intelligence.

2   **Past experience of the individual** : eg. when a hitherto comfort-loving and materialistic friend decides to sell all of his wordly goods, this would encourage an observer to look for unnoticed characteristics.

Laljee et al (1982) noted that explanations of unexpected behaviour were more complex than for expected behavour. Where the situation was unfamiliar and the behaviour unexpected explanations tended to be in terms of the situation. But where the situation was familiar and the behaviour unexpected, explanations tended to be in personality terms. We also tend to be selective about what we perceive about how a person behaves. This tendency is termed **'perceptual salience'**.

In an experiment by **Taylor et al (1979)** subjects were set to observe a discussion between six males. Under one condition they saw groups of five white men and one black, under the second three white and three black. The influence of the black man among the white was far stronger when he was alone among white men, than doing exactly the same things in a mixed group, ie. his behaviour carried more weight in the first condition.

McArthur and Post (1977) looked at sex composition in groups in a similar way and with similar findings.

Harvey et al (1975) showed that actions that result in a severe outcome - particularly if it is severe to the observer- results in more of the cause being located in the 'actor', eg. if you break a Ming vase worth £4,000 you are more likely to be thought clumsy or stupid than if you break a cup worth 50p.

In our selection of the information we observe about people, we tend to select that which justifies an **internal locus of cause,** and under-esti-mate or ignore situational influences. It seems very easy to make judge-ments of character to explain the behaviour we see, and the tendency is not to go beyond it.

A study by **Ross et al (1977)** illustrates this. They selected subjects for a game involving general knowledge, either as participants or as ob-servers. Participants were randomly allocated to the roles of question-ers or contestants. Questioners were requested to ask questions out of their own fund of general knowledge, providing they knew the answers. Contestants had to answer as best they could.

Afterwards, observers and questioners were asked to rate contestants on their general knowledge. In spite of the fact that questioners could display their knowledge while little opportunity was given for contestants to do the same, the latter received lower ratings, even from themselves.

Though there were fairly obvious external circumstances preventing contestants from displaying their knowledge, failure to do so was attributed to ignorance - ie. to an internal rather than an external cause.

Self assessment questions

1 Explain what is meant by 'locus of cause'.
2 Outline the three causes of behaviour dealt with by Jones and Davis and assess their implications for judgements of personality.
3 What did Kelley mean by 'distinctiveness', 'consistency' and 'consensus'?
4 What are some of the likely sources of error in attribution?
5 What is meant by 'perceptual salience'? How does it affect attribution?

SECTION III

ATTRACTION

We are all aware that there are some people we like and are attracted to; others we dislike. This section attempts to look at some of the factors that cause us become attracted to some people and not to others.

Social reinforcement

One of the factors that makes others attractive to us is their reward value to us. Different things are rewarding to different people. Some rewards might be :
(a) Help given by another.
(b) Esteem or approval.
(c) Physical appearance.

Our needs at a particular time also help to determine what is found to be rewarding. Someone whose self-confidence is low at a particular time might be attracted by someone who boosts his/her self-esteem.

The **reward value** of a person's behaviour also depends upon our evaluation of other factors to do with him/her. For example, we take into account the context in which the reward or reinforcement occurs. If someone is looking for a favour the fact that he/she is being very kind and helpful may not seem rewarding to us.

This **reward value** extends beyond the person who rewards us to anyone else who happens to be there, attraction may be generalised towards that person, and we will be attracted to that person as well.

This is well illustrated by a study by **Rabbie and Horowitz (1960)** who showed that even strangers brought together for a game-like task showed greater liking for each other when they were successful than when they were unsuccessful.

Byrne and Rhamey (1965) and **Hewitt (1972)** studied what they called the **'ingratiation effect'** and its opposite the **'extra credit effect'** (**Figure 2**). We tend to like those who evaluate us positively, and dislike those who evaluate us negatively. However, where the positive evaluation appears to us to be undeserved and we suspect that there may be an attempt at flattery, we tend to like the person less. Alternatively, a negative evaluation which we see as honest will tend to increase liking.

Figure 2 :

Ingratiation Effect

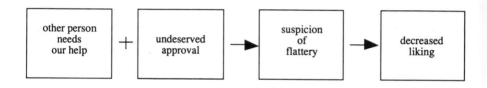

Extra Credit Effect

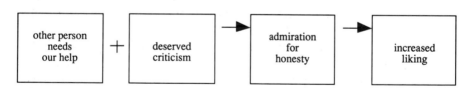

Sociograms

Within a group of people, individuals are asked which member of the group they prefer to associate with, spend their leisure time with and like. When these preferences are represented on a sociogram, we can easily see the patterns of liking or attraction that exist within the group, where the attractions are one-sided, where there are loners, and where some are very popular. A map can be produced to represent the people concerned indicating the direction of their preferences.

Figure 3 :

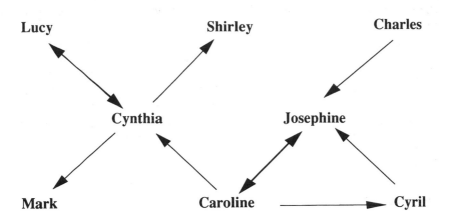

Example of a sociogram illustrating attractions between a group of eight.

In the above Figure 2 it can be clearly seen that Charles appears to be a loner with no-one expressing a preference for him, while Cynthia and Josephine are centres of attraction. The results of studies by this means show that popular individuals tend to be more attractive, healthier, better-off, better adjusted, more sociable, kinder, more competent at skills that are important to the group, than individuals that are less often chosen.

Aronson (1969) lists a number of factors that can influence choice of friends.

1 **Physical proximity :** We select friends, at least in part, on the basis of opportunity. **Festinger et al (1950)** found that the closer people lived together the more likely they were to become friends. Proximity increases the frequency of contact, and we tend to become attracted to those with whom we have frequent contact. **(Saergert et al, 1973)**

2 **Physical attractiveness :** Beautiful people are consistently chosen in preference to those of average appearance. This 'halo' effect makes us assume that attractive people are honest, intelligent, etc.

This association between beauty and attractiveness seems to apply more to women than to men. **Krebs and Adinolfs (1975)** studied the relationships between physical beauty and frequency of dating among college students and found a strong link. In marriage, attractive women seem most frequently to be paired with well-educated men with high incomes.

Berscheid and Walster (1974) suggested that this linking of beauty with choice preference was mostly on limited acquaintance. Later on, other personal qualities become important.

3 **Competence : Aronson (1969)** had college students listen to four tapes of candidates for the 'College Bowl'. This was a quiz competitition for general knowledge. On two of these tapes the person was represented as highly intelligent, and on the other two of only average ability. One of the 'intelligent' and one of the 'average' tapes included an incident where the candidate clumsily spilled coffee on himself. Of the four candidates, the one rated to be the most attractive was the intelligent but clumsy one, the least attractive the average and clumsy one. We seem to like our genius to be human.

4 **Similarity : Byrne (1969)** found that the more similar another person's attitudes were to our own the more we find ourselves attracted to him/her. Conversely, lack of similarity in attitudes makes us less likely to be attracted.

Newcombe (1961)in a study on similarity and attraction offered free board and lodging to intending university students in return for their participating in the study. In the few months preceding their university enrolment they lived together on campus. Similarity was found to be a good predictor of friendship choices, and that similarity increased as they got to know each other better. However, as with the majority of the studies mentioned here, the sample was not a typical one. They were students and they were male.

Homogamy

There seems to be a tendency to select as partners for marriage those who are similar in age, social class, religion and race. But then these are the people you will naturally come most into contact with, and it is likely that they will hold similar views and have much in common with you.

Hill, Rubin and Peplan (1976) followed 200 couples over a two year period. By this time half had broken up, but the other half were still going out, were engaged or were married. Correlations were made between couples on such attributes as **educational attainment, age, attractiveness, scholastic aptitude tests (SAT) and sex role traditionalism.** Those couples who stayed together were markedly more similar in these attributes than those who broke up.

Figure 4 :

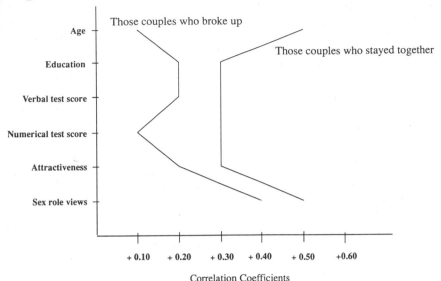

Those couples who broke up

Those couples who stayed together

| Age | Education | Verbal test score | Numerical test score | Attractiveness | Sex role views |

+ 0.10   + 0.20   + 0.30   + 0.40   + 0.50   +0.60

Correlation Coefficients

Homogomy (from Hill, Rubin and Peplan 1976)

The disputed question is whether homogamy is produced by the effects of similarity on liking, or whether it is merely a by- product of proximity. The third possibility is that we become more like the people that we spend a great deal of time with.

As **Berscheid and Walster (1978)** put it 'few of us have the opportunity to meet, interact with, or marry a person markedly dissimilar to ourselves'.

Izard (1960) looked at similarity of personality and attraction among first year girl students. Students who were initially strangers were asked to complete personality tests and then six months later to name the girls they liked best and least. He found a substantial similarity of personality between choosers and those they said they liked best and not with those they liked least.

Complementary needs theory

Winch Ktanes and Ktanes (1954) have stated that we are attracted by those whose personality complements our own. For example, a person who is dominant is likely to be attracted by one who is submissive. They interviewed a number of recently married couples to assess their personalities and found evidence of complementary needs. While this theory has considerable intuitive appeal there is little empirical support for it. **Katz Glucksberg and Krauss (1960)** did find some evidence of complemen-

19

tary needs but the needs they referred to were specifically related to the marital situation. And even in this context it seems to be contradicted by the work of **Cattell and Nesselroade (1967)** who found clear evidence that similarity in personality might be associated with a stable marital relationship.

It should be noted that the available research may be presenting an over-simplified picture of attraction. Few studies have considered individual differences among people - some may be attracted by similarity, others by complementarity.

Social exchange theory: (Thibault and Kelley 1978)

This is a rather mechanistic approach to attraction and interpersonal relationships. It regards behaviour as a commodity or a form of 'money' which we can invest in another person of our choice. It makes the assumption that we will work like businessmen to maximise our gains and minimise our costs.

Social exchange theory supposes that we will make an estimate of the rewards that accrue from interaction with person A or person B. They may each have their own set of rewards for us. Then, we estimate the costs attaching to each interaction. For example, a potential partner may be feckless so far as money matters are concerned - a cost - but a kind and loving person - a reward. Having weighed up the rewards and costs against the alternatives available to us, we settle for the alternative which yields us the best 'profit'. This evaluation of costs and rewards cannot be done in a vacuum. We have to have a standard of comparison - a 'comparison level' - and not only that, but also a comparison level for alternatives.

Both partners have to emerge from the interaction with a profit in order for the interaction to continue. The outcome in each person's case will be rewards minus costs. In addition, each party has to bear in mind that any interaction will mean foregoing some other interaction with its attendant rewards and costs, and we have to judge whether it is worth it.

Whenever two persons judge that the outcomes are the best that they can achieve in the circumstances, the interaction proceeds - but only so long as it remains profitable for both of them.

Figure 5 :

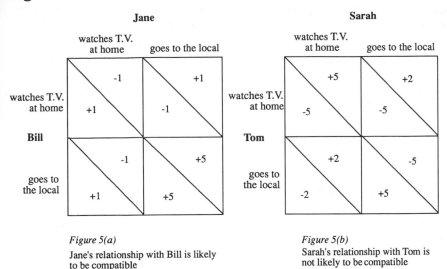

Figure 5(a)
Jane's relationship with Bill is likely
to be compatible

Figure 5(b)
Sarah's relationship with Tom is
not likely to be compatible

Social Exchange Theory (Thibaut and Kelly 1978)

The costs and rewards attaching to an interaction have been illustrated by a matrix (Figure 5).

Attempts are made to put figures on to the costs and rewards involved so that it can be seen clearly which behaviour on the part of each person yields rewards and which costs. Then so long as each person behaves in a way that is rewarding to the other, and without too great cost the relationship will flourish.

An evaluation of social exchange theory :

1   There is an inherent difficulty in attempting to define rewards or quantify costs for any particular individual. Any test of the theory is likely to involve a great deal of speculation.

2   The central assumption that people always make choices solely on the basis of personal satisfaction is hard to maintain. In some societies, for instance, relationships are controlled by social norms outside an individual's control.

However, it is useful to apply the theory to some of the other factors which have been seen to affect the attractiveness to us of others. Take similarity in beliefs, values and attitudes for example. Kendel suggests we prefer to associate with those who are similar to ourselves. But the costs of interaction with those whose understanding of the world is different from ours is likely to be great.

As we have already noted, physical attractiveness is greatly valued, especially in women. Intelligence also has a considerable value in our culture. Our tendency, therefore, is to invest our resources in those who are physically attractive, intelligent, well-adjusted, happy and outgoing. We would, if we could, interact only with these people. However, whether we succeed in this depends on what we ourselves have to offer. It may be that one settles for a compromise; this probably means someone of similar attractiveness to oneself.

Self assessment questions

1 What is meant by **'social reinforcement'**?

2 What is meant by the **'ingratiation effect'** and the **'extra- credit effect'**?

3 What factors does Aronson suggest as influencing our choice of friends?

4 Can it reasonably be said that we like people who are similar to ourselves?

5 How valuable do you consider **social exchange theory** to be as an explanation of our choices of people to interact with? What are its limitations?

SECTION IV

NATURE OF PREJUDICE

Allport (1954) defines prejudice as :
'An antipathy based upon a faulty and inflexible generalisation directed towards a group as a whole or towards an individual because he is a member of that group. It may be felt or experienced.'
   Prejudice can be seen as a strong tendency to be unfairly hostile to someone on the basis of his/her racial, ethnic, religious, political or even sexual attributes and to act towards him/her in a discriminatory or hostile manner.
As with all attitudes, prejudice has three components :

1 **Cognitive** - beliefs and perceptions through which we form stereotypes which cause us to over-generalise about individuals on the basis of their group membership.

2 **Affective** - feelings of hostility, often intense, which may serve as an ego defence.

3 **Behavioural** - a tendency to act in a discriminatory manner towards a person or a group. This takes a very broad range of forms, from verbal denigration - including racial jokes - to the genocide which

resulted from prejudice against Jews in Nazi Germany.
Prejudice goes beyond discrimination against minority groups and can include such things as the problems of introducing farm machinery in India, or the acceptance of contraception for women. Sometimes it involves the dominant minority - as in South Africa - showing prejudice against the majority group.

Causes of prejudice

Stereotyping (see also section 1)

The need of human beings to categorise their environment and predict outcomes on the basis of minimal cues leads to the perceptual and cognitive process of stereotyping. We assign certain characteristics to a particular group. On meeting members of that group we expect them to share these characteristics.

This is a neutral process which fulfils an important function in our daily life. The stereotypes we hold of a group may equally be favourable as unfavourable.

This process has been well documented in research. **Katz and Braly (1933)** and later **Gilbert (1951)** presented Princeton undergraduates with a list of 84 character traits and asked them to indicate which were the most characteristic of several racial or ethnic groups - Jews, Chinese, Negroes etc. There was strong agreement on the perceived characteristics of these groups. Later studies, such as that by **Karlins, Coffman and Walters (1969)** found that stereotyping persisted though the content of many of the stereotypes had changed. (See Section I, p.8)

Social judgement theory

Holding extreme views which are important to our self-image causes us to perceive discrepant views as more opposed to our own than in fact they are. **(Reference : Attitude Changes : Chapter 3)** Prejudice is essentially evaluative. We make up our minds about the characteristics of those we are prejudiced against and when we come across an individual who does not conform to these characteristics he is regarded as untypical.

Social attitudes

In some views, prejudice stems from specific traits of personality which predispose an individual to react with hostility towards ethnic, racial, political or religious or other minority groups.

Adorno et al (1950) identified what they called the **'authoritarian personality'** whose characteristics are as follows:

1   He/she has great concern for authority relationships, showing deference to his superiors and dominating those below him - 'the bicyclist's personality' 'above they bow, below they kick'.

2   He adheres strictly to the rules of society, shows great respect for conventional behaviour, values and morality, and is aggressive towards those who flout these values.

3   He is anti-introspective and tough-minded and preoccupied by the division between the weak and the strong.

4   He is egocentric and rigid in his thought process.

5   He denies his own immoral feelings but suspects immoral behaviour in others especially of a sexual nature. He is convinced of his own rightness and of the decadence around him.

6   He is cynical about the human race and exploits others, whilst complaining about being exploited himself. He has both sadistic and masochistic tendencies.

7   He is intensely prejudiced and intolerant towards minority groups.

Eysenck (1953) found evidence for a strongly anti-semitic social attitude; 31 per cent of his middle class sample believed that Jews in their dealings with others are 'an absolute menace, money grabbing and unscrupulous'.

Rokeach (1960) extended this concept of **authoritarianism** further. To him it is **'dogmatism'** which he defines as **'closed-mindedness'**. The dogmatic person works from a set of highly organised attitudes usually derived from authority in some form, which are extremely resistant to change in the face of new information. He can equally well be politically right or left wing. **Eysenck (1954, 1957)** also, in his Social Attitudes Inventory, suggests that authoritarianism exists both on the left and the right.

Fenkel-Brunswick and Sandford (1949) in their study of University sorority members found evidence of similar personality characteristics as well as much suppressed hostility and aggression beneath a front of conventional behaviour and deference to the social norms of their group.

Scapegoat theory

The proposition is that frustration leads to aggression. When the legitimate target of that aggression is inaccessible, it will be diverted on to targets where it is condoned or encouraged. For example, a person who is unable to get a job may blame it on the large number of immigrants in the area.

Weatherley (1961) divided subjects according to their scores on an anti-semitism scale. Half the subjects were subjected to very insulting remarks while filling in a questionnaire. Then they were given picture-story tests, that is, they were asked to tell a story about each of a series of pictures.

Some of the pictures showed people with Jewish sounding names. Analysis of the data showed that subjects high on anti-semitism directed more aggression towards the Jewish pictures than those low on anti-semitism. The experimenter lowered the self-esteem of the subjects by insulting them when they could do little about it. The aggression that resulted found a target in a group that was already disliked. This study clearly has ethical implications. Is it right to lower subjects' self esteem in this way? Is it doing them permanent damage?

Scapegoat theory has limitations though. It does nothing to explain the prejudice of minorities towards majorities - as in South Africa - there is no frustration here. Or, for example, the prejudice of a peasant woman against contraception.

Exploitation theory

This has its origins in Marxist philosophy. Prejudice is seen as propagated by an exploiting class to stigmatize some groups as inferior to justify continued exploitation. It fits neatly into a larger theory of social relations, but it is doubtful whether it could stand on its own.

Socio-cultural determinants

A wide range of sociological factors have been seen to contribute to the establishment and the maintenance of prejudice. These include the following :

1   **Density of population :** It has been shown that where population is densest, prejudice is most common.

2   **Community separations:** The creation of ghettos, or the separation of minorities into particular areas of cities can foster prejudice.

3   **Ignorance and barriers to communication :** Language barriers or ignorance about cultural differences are seen as providing a cause of prejudice.

4   **Ease of vertical mobility :** Where it is easy to move upwards there tends to be competition and jealousy of the position reached. This can lead to barriers being erected of race perhaps, or culture or class.

5   **Rapid changes in social structure :** Similarly, rapid changes in society lead to jockeying for position. Incomers can be resented.

6   **Competition for employment :** In times of high unemployment members of ethnic minorities can be seen as competing unfairly for the jobs that the indigenous population consider rightfully to be theirs.

7   **Importation of cheap labour :** Where cheap labour has been brought in to fill a need, resentment can grow towards the incomers when that need no longer exists. Large numbers of Turks and Jugoslavs were brought into Germany to supply a labour shortage. This shortage has now become a dearth of jobs and the foreign labour that settled there has become an object of prejudice.

Pettigrew (1958) believes that conformity to the dominant group norms is a critical factor in prejudice.

Anti-black prejudice in the United States and in South Africa was related to measures of general conformity to group norms. The need to conform and not deviate from the norms of the group was paramount.

This, however, goes further to explain the maintenance of an existing prejudice than the cause of prejudice arising.

When one's self appears to be threatened there seems to be a need to externalise the blame and contempt by prejudiced behaviour towards others.

Attemps to reduce prejudice

Research has focused upon diminishing those factors which maintain and legitimise prejudice.

1   Increasing contact between members of groups

The opportunity to interact is asociated with increases in living standards. As people interact and know each other more, the more they should see each other as similar.

Secord and Backman (1974) found that increased interaction does decrease prejudice but only in the context in which the meeting takes place. Generalisation to other situations is minimal.

2   Interdependance of behavior

This is a common attempt to overcome an external obstacle or enemy by co-operation with others. **Star, Williams and Stouffe (1958)** showed that soldiers who fought together in the war showed less prejudice towards minority group members. In **Sherif's (1961)** study, hostility among young boys was reduced by having them co-operate in removing frustrating obstacles. In this well-known study Sherif and his co-workers investigated the effects upon groups of young boys in a summer camp of artificially manipulating group attitudes. The boys were initially allowed to associate and make friends with others in their own tents. Then their friendships were arbitrarily broken up by the assignment of the boys to groups named 'Bulldogs' and 'Red Devils'. These first lived and worked separately, then were pitted against one another with the result that prejudice arose

26

between the groups. This hostility was eventually reduced by having the boys co-operate in removing obstacles that had been found to be frustrating.

Legislation

Sexism

Sexism is a particular form of prejudice which results in males being given an advantage in terms of social and material advancement simply because they are male. **Treisman and Terrell (1975)** showed that for every dollar a man earned a woman was paid just 75 cents.

Bem (1975) suggested that the healthiest state of mind was that of androgyny - that is where a person has both masculine and feminine traits.

Jacklin and Maccoby (1978) have indicated that while there appear to be different cognitive styles between men and women, the people who are most successful seem to be those who combine male and female styles, who are in the middle of a continuum of masculinity and femininity.

At all events, the goal of reducing and eliminating the dominance of men and consequently of masculine styles of operating seems likely to have as its result an overall improvement in cognitive social and emotional functioning.

Attempts have been made to reduce prejudice by means of legislation, though this tends to tackle the symptoms rather than the root causes of prejudice.

Self assessment questions

1 What arc the nature and components of prejudice?
2 What is meant by the **'Authoritarian Personality'**? What bearing has this personality trait upon prejudice?
3 What is **'Scapegoat'** theory in relation to prejudice? What are its limitations?
4 What are some of the **socio-cultural** factors that have been suggested as causes of prejudice?
5 Describe some of the approaches to the problem of reducing prejudice. How far are they successful?

Further Reading :

Judy Gahagan (1984) **Social Interaction and its Management** London Methuen New Essential Psychology Series Ch. 6.
Henri Tajfel and Colin Fraser (eds) (1978) **Introducing Social Psychology** Harmondsworth Penguin Books Ch.9.

" SPEED, A QUICK START, COMFORTABLE SUSPENSION — EVERYTHING PROVES IT'S MUCH BETTER THAN THE ONE I **NEARLY** BOUGHT ! "

Chapter 3

Attitudes

At the end of this chapter you should be able to :

1   Describe what is meant by the term 'attitude', state some definitions of the word and identify the main components of an attitude.

2   Show some of the ways in which attitudes may be formed and developed.

3   Describe and make some evaluation of the main approaches that have been adopted to the measurement of attitudes.

4   Describe some of the studies that have been conducted into the role communication and persuasion in bringing about attitude change.

5   Describe and evaluate some of the theories that have been developed to explain the way in which attitudes change, including dissonance theory and the application of attribution theory to this area.

SECTION I

DEVELOPMENT FORMATION AND MEASUREMENT

Beliefs, Values and Attitudes

Fishbein and Ajzen (1975) distinguished **attitudes** from **beliefs**. Beliefs form links between objects and attributes, eg. 'Russia is a totalitarian state'. The object 'Russia' is linked to an attribute 'totalitarian state'. They are distinguished from attitudes in that they are not in themselves evaluative. There is no indication in this statement whether totalitarian states are a good or bad thing. However, attitudes are evaluative. A statement of an attitude might be something like the following:

'People are unhappy in a totalitarian state'. 'Unhappy' is an evaluative adjective.

Values are the premises or assumptions from which attitudes come. They are what we regard as important. 'Better dead than red' might be a value statement and indicate the value we place upon Communist ideals. They are therefore highly evaluative and closely related to attitudes. We maintain a favourable attitude to anything which helps promote our values.

Attitudes are 'learned predispositions to respond in a consistently favourable or unfavourable way towards a given object, person or event' (**Fishbein and Ajzen, 1975**). Other definitions include that of **Krech, Crutchfield and Ballachey (1962)** :

'**Attitudes** are enduring systems of positive or negative evaluations, emotional feelings and pro and con action techniques with respect to social objectives'.

Osgood, Suci and Tannenbaum (1957) :

'**Attitudes** are predispositions to respond, but are distinguished from other states of readiness in that they predispose towards an evaluative response'.

Smith, Bruner and White (1956) :

'An **attitude** is a predisposition to experience, to be motivated by and to act towards a class of objects in a predictable way.'

The components of an attitude

Attitudes are widely held to have three components, **cognitive, affective** and **behavioural.**

An individual's responses to an object may be of three kinds :

(i) **Cognitive responses** - eg, perceptions of something or reports of beliefs. For example: "an airport nearby is noisy, and will cause danger".

(ii) **Affective responses** - feelings or motivations, prompted by the object. For example: "an airport nearby will cause me anxiety and I hate it".

(iii) **Behavioural or conative responses** - behavioural responses relating to an object, or else behavioural intentions. For example: "I intend to lobby parliament to prevent this airport being constructed here".

Figure 6 :

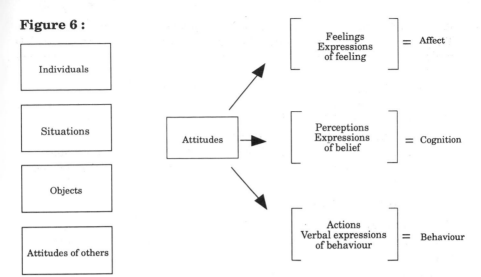

**Schematic Conception of Attitudes
(From Rosenberg and Hovand 1960)**

In other words, attitudes are fairly permanent sets of evaluations which we carry around with us and which have the effect of colouring the interpretations we make of the people and things we meet and so make us more predictable in our responses than we otherwise might be. They affect our feelings, our perceptions and our behaviour towards a wide range of objects, people and events. It is, therefore, important to consider how they are formed and how they may come to be changed.

For example, I might have a hostile attitude towards amusement arcades in seaside resorts. This attitude will have the effect of actually making that arcade off the seafront appear to me noisier, more obtrusive and more vulgar. This may well make me take a dislike to that area of the town where the arcade is, so that I will avoid it whenever I can. My cognitive response is to make it noisier, my affective response will make me dislike it and my conative response makes me avoid it.

Attitude formation

Attitudes seem to be learned predispositions to behave in a particular way towards an object or a person, but there is some debate about the way in which the learning takes place. Some of the approaches to this are outlined over leaf.

Classical conditioning of attitudes

Zanna, Kiessler and Pilkonis (1970) conducted two apparently unrelated studies, run by different experimenters. Subjects received electric shocks so that their physiological reactions might be monitored. The words 'light' and 'dark' were paired with the onset and the end of the shock - a negative and a positive event.

In a second study attitudes to various words were assessed, including 'light' and 'dark' and also related words such as 'white' and 'black' together with unrelated words used as a control. Words that had signalled shock onset and related words were evaluated more negatively than neutral control words. Words signalling shock ending and words relating to these, were evaluated more positively than the control. However, the study as it was conducted seems very far removed from the way in which attitudes might be conditioned in everyday life by the positive or negative stimuli that accompany them. But it does seem to show that there are circumstances in which attitudes might be classically conditioned.

Information processing and attitudes

Petty and Caccioppo (1981) claim that attitudes are formed through increasing familiarity with an object. With increasing familiarity, we move from what they describe as **'descriptive beliefs'** - largely matters of perceived fact - to **'inferential beliefs'**. We make an inspired guess about what the beliefs might be. It is from these 'inferential beliefs' that attitudes are formed.

Figure 7 :

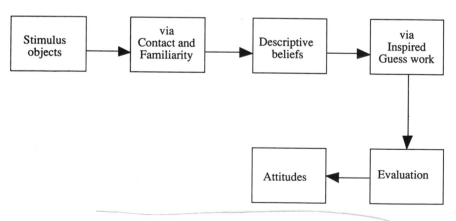

An Information Processing Model of Attitude Formation (From Petty and Caccioppo 1981)

32

Nature/nurture and attitudes

It seems manifestly unlikely that attitudes are innate. There are so many examples of a conflict in attitudes between generations. However, there does seem to be some evidence that some aspects of personality are innate. Eysenck claims that his stability/neuroticism dimension of personality is genetically transmitted. **(Eysenck, 1981)** It seems likely that such personality traits will have an influence on the formation of attitudes in a person. Equally, aspects of personality may be learned, and this learning may be influenced by genetic factors. While attitudes may be influenced by genetic factors, specific attitudes have their origin in experience. Imitation seems likely to be a way in which attitudes are acquired.

Bandura and McDonald (1953) attempted to demonstrate this. Children were told pairs of stories. In both stories in the pair there were acts involving damage - a selfish act involving minimal damage and unselfish act resulting in considerable damage. The children were asked to say which of the acts was naughtier. Their responses were evaluated and then the children were exposed to one of two conditions

(i) Some observed adults expressing attitudes contrary to their own

(ii) Others did not observe adults, but were reinforced when they expressed attitudes contrary to their original ones.

They were then re-tested on the pairs of stories to see if changes of attitude had occurred. The reinforcement condition resulted in far less change in attitude than the imitation condition.

In an earlier study **Horowitz (1936)** showed pictures of black and white children to groups of children of different ages and asked them to pick out from the pictures the children they would like to

(i) take home

(ii) play ball with

(iii) join their play group

While the younger children showed no over-all pattern of preference older children became with age increasingly similar in their responses. Situational influences seemed to become less important as the children grew older and they developed an over- all set of attitudes (either positive or negative) towards coloured children.

Measurement of attitudes

Attitudes are not directly observable and so attitude measures tend to concentrate on one or other of the components: **cognitive, affective or**

behavioural. (See above, page 30)

The Thurstone scale of attitude measurement (1929) attempts to measure the cognitive component. Thurstone assembled a set of 130 statements representing both favourable and unfavourable attitudes. These statements were then given to a large number of judges to arrange them into 11 categories labelled A - K. F represented a neutral position. The 20 statements which had the greatest agreement from the judges then constituted the final scale. Each was given a value. This was arrived at by averaging all the judges ratings. The subject was then presented with the statements in a random order and asked to indicate those that he/she agreed with. When the numerical values attached to these statements were averaged the experimenters could obtain a measure of the subject's attitude.

There are some problems with this method, quite apart from the very cumbersome procedure of assembling the very large numbers of judges to rate vast numbers of attitudinal statements. First, the subject ticks those statements he/she agrees with, so that it is perfectly possible for two subjects to end up with the same attitude score while endorsing a very different set of statements. The values attached to the statements are likely to be dependent on the judges used. Thurstone's argument that the judges would be objective in their sorting was not supported by a study by **Hovland and Sherif (1952)** who found that there was a definite bias in the way that Negro and pro-Negro judges sorted statements of attitudes to Negroes as compared to anti-Negro judges.

Finally, Thurstone assumed that data from an attitude scale was **interval** level data, eg. a score of 6 is three times as favourable as a score of 2. Given that judges' ratings may not be totally objective, do we perhaps have only an ordinal scale - that is, all we have done is put people into a rank order?

Likert Scale (1932). This is probably the most widely used measure of attitudes, and it also deals with the cognitive component. Here, the subject chooses his own degree of agreement with a set of attitude statements and a numerical value is attached to this degree of agreement. For example, a statement such as 'The abolition of the death penalty has led to an increase in all kinds of violence' would be accompanied by an invitation to the subject to show his degree of agreement by endorsing one of the following

1   strongly agree

2   agree

3   undecided

4   disagree

5   strongly disagree

the numbers in brackets being the numerical value attached to that degree of agreement, which would not, of course, be included in the statement as presented to the subjects. The total score is the sum of all the values, which the subject has attached to all the items on the scale. Half the items would be constructed to represent a 'pro' attitude and the other half a 'con' attitude and the scoring would be altered accordingly. Again, as with the Thurstone scale, there is the possibility that a different pattern of responding might produce the same over-all score and as with the Thurstone scale, it only yields an ordinal scale measurement. However, it does have the virtue of much greater simplicity.

Osgood's Semantic Differential

This attempts to measure the affective component in attitudes. It approaches this by means of an assessment of the connotative meanings of words, that is, the subjective feeling that attaches to words. The way Osgood achieves this is first to assemble a set of at least nine bi-polar adjectives - good—bad, strong— weak, active—passive. The adjectives used need to include those that illustrate three main factors which he claimed made up each concept represented by the word :

evaluative   ie good—bad

potency   ie strong—weak

activity   ie active—passive

Between each pair of adjectives is a seven point scale with a neutral mid-point. Subjects are asked to indicate with an X which of the poles represent to them the meaning of the word and how closely, viz :

Figure 8 :

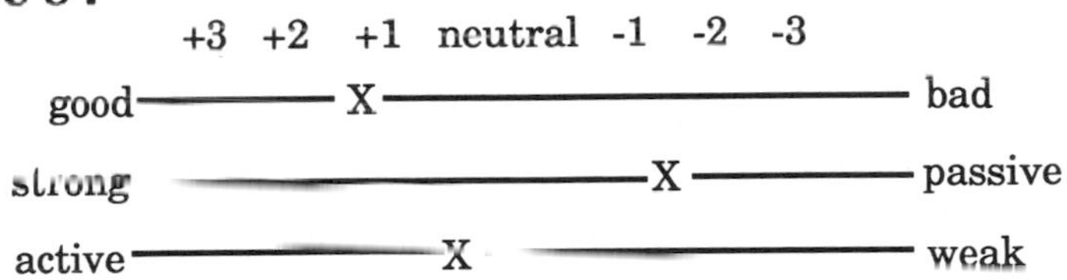

```
        +3  +2  +1  neutral  -1  -2  -3
  good————————X—————————————————— bad
  strong ———————————————————X——————— passive
  active————————————X————————————— weak
```

(from Osgood, Suci and Tannenbaum, 1957)

An individual's score is the total on all the scales for the concept. The difficulties involved with this are not only that it is very subjective There is no allowance made for response bias. A subject may always employ the extreme ends of the scale or always tend towards the neutral point. In addition, it is not clear what the neutral point indicates when a subject marks that. Is it that he does not care, does not know or perhaps that he cannot make up his mind? Most responses represent a complex set of evaluations, which the differential is not really adequate to represent. **(Osgood, Suci and Tannenbaum, 1957)**

Social Distance Scale

Bogardus attempted with his **Social Distance Scale (1925)** to measure the conative or behavioural component of attitudes, that is to say, the intentions of the subject or his actions.

Subjects were asked to indicate from seven statements indicating degrees of intimacy which were acceptable to them in relation to the person in question. These levels included such things as :

(1)   to close kinship by marriage

(2)   as visitors only to my country

(3)   would exclude from my country

The values attached to these statements can provide a numerical representation of the attitude of the subject.

This technique is obviously quite limited in application though **Triandis (1971)** has used it quite extensively to measure attitudes to religion and race. It is quite useful as a simple tool but the stimuli in question are normally negatively perceived by the subjects and the technique only shows the degree of acceptance of this negative stimulus.

Sociometry also has been used to measure the behavioural or cognitive components of attitudes. It has already been described in Chapter 2 (page 17). In any group, members are asked such questions as 'Who would you most like to sit next to?' 'Who would you like to go on holiday with?' 'Who do you want to work with?'. The responses to such questions are mapped to indicate those who are over- or under-chosen.

Pushkin (1967) used the technique with three to seven year old children to study their ethnic choices in play situations. He used black and white dolls in a tea party situation. The hostess was represented by a white doll, there were five chairs and ten dolls - black and white. The child was asked to place them on chairs round the table. Thus she was allowed either to accept or to reject, maybe on ethnic grounds. Other similar tests employed by Pushkin included the **'see-saw test'**, where the child had to choose from mixed dolls the one that should sit on the other end of the see-saw, and the **'house test'** which allows children to express preferences on ethnic grounds as to who they wanted as neighbours.

The problems thrown up by these tests include the following :

(i)   The problem of answering so as to appear in the best light - this is a problem common to a wide range of personality tests where one response is seen as more socially desirable than another.

(ii) They give no indication of why an attitude is held, only that it is and possibly how strongly.

(iii) Where there are two tests of attitudes to what extent do the responses on the first influence the responses on the second? The tests themselves may have a hand in 'making' attitudes.

(iv) We may not be aware of our attitudes. Even honest answers may not reflect real attitudes.

A further approach to the problem has been the development of **projective techniques.** Ambiguous stimuli are presented to the subjects on which they can project their attitudes. The **Thematic Apperception Tests** developed by **Murray** in the 1930's are an example. Others include **Rorschach Ink Blot Tests.** In the former pictures are shown to the subject and he/she is asked to write an account of what is happening in the picture. These are then interpreted by skilled professionals and attitudes are identified. In the latter, coloured ink blots are the stimuli and the subject is invited to put down his/her impressions.

Self assessment questions

1 What are some of the definitions of attitudes? How may we distinguish between values, beliefs and attitudes.

2 Outline some of the ways it has been suggested that attitudes are formed.

3 What are some of the approaches to attitude measurement? What are their limitations?

SECTION II

ATTITUDE CHANGE

It is necessary to examine also the way in which attitudes change and some of the factors that may influence this change. These include :

(i) Persuasive Communication

This is the way in which a communication occurs between two people resulting in a change in attitude. If the communication has been successful - the message has got through - then attitude change occurs. McGuire (1969) saw the processes concerned in this persuasive communication as the sequence in Figure 9 overleaf.

Figure 9 :

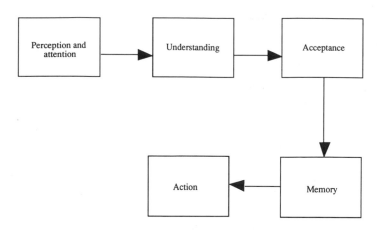

Process of Persuasive Communication
(from Mc Guire 1968)

Researchers have looked at each stage of the process to identify the way in which they affect the outcome - the amount of persuasion, ie. the amount of attitude change.

Most of the work on persuasive communications has originated from the **"Yale Communication and Attitude Change Programme"** of the 1950's under **Hovland** and his colleagues. The Yale researchers studied the following aspects of communication as independent variables in the experimental context. The dependent variables in each case were the success of the communication, the amount of attitude change that resulted

The process of a communication will involve three components - the source of the message, the message itself and the receiver of the message. The variables studied by the Yale group included each of these :

Source variables   ie   the perceived characeristics of the source of the message

Message variables   ie   the content and structure of the message

Receiver variables   ie. the characteristics of those who receive the message

That is :
   WHO?
   SAYS WHAT?
   TO WHOM?

We shall examine each of these in turn.

Source variables - Who?

Among source variables studied are the following :

(i)   communicator credibility

(ii) communicator expertise

(iii) intentions or motives

(iv) attractiveness

(1) **Communicator credibility** : this involves the over-all believability of the source.

In a study by **Kelman and Hovland (1953)** subjects were asked to listen to a message which advocated more lenient treatment of juvenile offenders .

The source of the message was ostensibly in one case

(i)   A prestigious juvenile court judge (high credibility)

or

(ii) An alleged drug-pedlar (low credibility)

Immediately afterwards subjects' attitudes were assessed.   The high-credibility source (the judge) was found to be more persuasive than the low credibility source (the alleged drug-pedlar). This is not surprising.

Three weeks later attitudes were re-assessed and half the subjects were reminded who the source of the message was.

The results showed that

(1)   Where there was no reminder there was a significant decrease in persuasion in the high-credibility condition and a small (non-significant) increase in the low-credibility condition.

(2)   Where there was a reminder the original results were maintained.

Hovland argued from this that the connection between the arguments and the conclusion of the message was remembered longer than the connection between the **'cue' - eg, communicator credibility** and the content of the message.   The cues became dissociated from the message over time.   This has become known as the **'sleeper effect'**.

Later research by **Gillig and Greenwald (1974)** seems to have cast doubt upon this effect, though.

(2) **Expertise :** If we believe someone is an expert - even in a different field - we tend to believe him. **Hovland and Weiss (1951)**compared a low credibility source (a mass circulation paper) and a high credibility source (a reputable medical journal) in each case dealing with a critical issue such as drugs.   The high credibility source achieved 22.5 per cent attitude

change on a pre- and post-test, the low credibility source only 8.4 per cent.

(3) **Intentions or motives:** The perceived motives of the source also can have an effect. **Walster and Festinger (1962)** compared the effectiveness of an 'overheard' message to one that was directed at the subjects in the usual way.

The **overheard message** was found to be more effective in changing attitudes but only where there was a high personal involvement, eg. the message that husbands should spend more time at home was more effective with married than with single women.

(4) **Attractiveness :** Where the source is perceived as attractive to the receiver there seems to be greater persuasability. **Similarity** is one aspect of this attractiveness. Others are **physical attractiveness** and **liking or disliking.** Though there is evidence **(Zimbardo, 1960: Brehm and Cohen, 1962)** that a disliked source can be more persuasive than an admired one.

Message Attributes - Says what?

(1) Confidence and Uncertainty

Maslow, Yoselson and London (1971) attempted to show whether the manner in which a message is delivered has a decisive influence upon whether it is believed.

Subjects were presented with written documentation of a law case to enable them to decide whether the accused seemed to be guilty or innocent. Before they decided, they were asked to study an argument in favour of the accused. Although the content of the message was the same in each case

(1) Under one condition the arguments were presented **confidently** - with statements like 'Obviously, I believe' - and 'I am quite sure'.

(2) Under the second condition the arguments were more **tentatively** presented with statements such as 'I don't know' - and 'I am not positive' - and 'I am unsure'.

The number of subjects agreeing with the counsel for the defence was significantly higher where the message was put forward in a confident verbal manner.

A second experiment using an actor putting forward arguments orally in a confident, neutral or doubtful manner found similar results.

(2) Fear Arousal

The first experimental study on the effects of fear arousal and persuasion was conducted by Janis and Feshback (1953).

The topic chosen was dental hygiene. Specific recommendations were included as to how and when it should be performed. There were three conditions of fear arousal :

(1) **Strong fear appeal** - much greater emphasis was placed upon the pain from toothache - including pain from dental treatment that might result from not observing the recommendations.

(2) **Moderate fear appeal condition** - where there was less emphasis upon the pain resulting from not observing the recommendations.

(3) **Mild fear appeal condition** - where there was least emphasis upon the fear arousal.

There was also a control condition where subjects received a talk on a different topic.

On a measurement of reported changes in tooth brushing practices and visits to dentists, the strong fear appeal group did not differ in any way from the control group. Only the mild fear appeal group conformed significantly more than the control. The experimenters concluded that 'the evidence strongly suggests that as the amount of fear arousing material is increased, conformity to the recommended actions tends to decrease'.

The dependent variable here is behaviour rather than attitude and this might account for the results. Part of the talk was concerned with a discussion of the proper type of toothbrush to use. A subsequent question-naire showed that all three experimental groups have shown a significant change in acceptance of the conclusions of the discussion.

Leventhal et al (1965) found contrasting results. A high degree of fear led to a greater attitude change. The subject was tetanus and the need for anti-tetanus innoculation. While great fear arousal led to greater attitude change, it did not lead to greater behavioural change in having innocula-tion. However, it could be said that tetanus is seen as a much more serious matter than dental hygiene.

(3) One-sided or two-sided presentation

Is it more effective to present both sides of an argument or one side only?

Hovland, Lusdaine and Sheffield (1949) using mass propaganda to change soldiers' attitudes found that it depended upon the level of educa-tion of the recipients. Better educated soldiers tended to be influenced more by two-sided, less educated by one-sided communication. Also those whose attitude was initially similar to the message were more affected by a one-sided message.

(4) Primacy or Recency Effects

Does the order of presentation of two opposing arguments effect the persuasion achieved.

Hovland (1957) drew the following conclusions :

1   The first communication was likely to be more effective **(primacy effect)** if both sides of the argument are presented by the same person and subjects are not initially **aware** that conflicting arguments will be

put forward.

2   The primacy effect was also evident when the subject has a degree of public commitment at the end of the presentation of the first message.

(5) Explicit or implicit conclusions

Hovland and Mandel (1952) showed that explicit conclusions drawn by persuaders at the end of the their message tend to be more effective. **McGuire (1968)** explains this finding by saying that subjects may not be intelligent enough or motivated enough to draw the conclusions for themselves.

Receiver attributes - To whom

(1) Intra- personal factors

These include

1   the initial attitude of the subject on the topic in question

2   the personal involvement of the subject with topic

Sherif and Hovland (1961) proposed a theory that a person's position on an attitude scale serves as an anchor from which he perceives and evaluates other positions on the attitude scale.

Where a communicator advocates a position close to that of the subject, the position will be seen as closer to his own than it is in reality (**assimilation**). Where the communicator advocates a distant position, it is seen as being even more distant (**contrast**).

Statements within the **assimilation** area represent the **latitude of acceptance** and those outside the **latitude of rejection.** The width of these latitudes of acceptance or rejection depend upon :

1   the extremeness of the subject's initial position

2   the degree of ego-involvement with the topic

The more extreme the initial position, and the more the egoinvolvement, the wider the latitude of rejection. (**Sherif, Sherif and Nebergall, 1965**)

Where there is a very wide latitude of rejection the only method of persuasion is to adopt a step-by-step technique - to present a message near enough to the subject's position to be within his latitude of acceptance - then proceed to the next step.

(2) Personality factors

Are some people more easily persuaded than others regardless of the topic or other variables? Persuasibility seems to be a personality variable on its own account.

Attitude change involves :

1   Comprehension of the message

2   Acceptance of it (yielding to the position of the communicator) (**McGuire, 1968**)

(McGuire, 1968)
Intelligence would make it more likely that some comprehension would occur but an intelligent person might be more confident of his own position so that he might be less likely to yield.

Self-esteem on the other hand would make it less likely that yielding would occur.

Anxiety: An anxious person might be more likely to yield but his anxiety might make it more difficult for him to comprehend the message.

Although there has been a great deal of research into this area, there are not many firm conclusions drawn.

More recent research on the way persuasion comes about in relation to the receiver of the message centres on the fact that attitudes seem sometimes to change even when not much thought is being given to the issue in question **(Miller, Maruyama, Beaber and Valone, 1976)**. But the amount of thought that is given to a discussion will affect the endurance of the attitude change. **Petty and Caccioppo (1979)** argued that there were two basic routes to persuasion, **central route processing** in which attitudes are changed while a person is motivated to think carefully about some thing and **peripheral route processing,** where attitudes are changed even though motivation to think about the issue is very low **(Cooper and Croyle, 1984)**. The central route might be taken for example after carefully listening to a persuasive argument and this is likely to be a change that lasts. However, a change in attitude that comes about after - for instance - noticing that a TV advertisement has a pleasant jingle and nice looking people is likely to take the peripheral route and to be much more temporary. **(Cialdini, Levy, Herman, Kozlowki and Petty, 1976)** A study by **Chaiken (1980)** demonstrated the importance of these two routes. Subjects were exposed to a message that contained either two or six arguments in favour of a particular position. Half the subjects - the **central route condition** - were told that they would be interviewed about the issue and so had the motivation to pay close attention to it. The other half - **the peripheral route condition** - were told they would be interviewed on an unrelated issue and so had much less motivation to pay attention to the arguments. The central processing group showed attitude change that was determined primarily by the number of arguments employed. Six arguments had a greater effect than two. It did not matter whether the speaker was liked or not. The other group showed that it did matter whether they liked the speaker or not, but the number of arguments presented made no difference. Furthermore a second measurement of attitudes taken ten days later showed the attitudes of the central processing group were much more stable than those of the peripheral processing group.

1   What stages does McGuire suggest a subject has to go through before he is persuaded to change his attitude?

2   What factors have been studied by the Yale University researchers relating to

(i)   the source of a message

(ii) the message itself and the way it is presented

(iii) the receiver of the message

3   What conclusions did they reach?

SECTION III

DISSONANCE AND BALANCE

This approach to attitude change makes the assumption that we like our beliefs, attitudes and behaviours to be consistent. Where there is an inconsistency between the way we behave and our beliefs and attitudes then we are uncomfortable, and are motivated to reduce the inconsistency. Perhaps the most important investigations in this area have been those of Festinger, who developed a theory of **Cognitive Dissonance. (Festinger, 1957).**

Briefly stated, his theory maintains that where there is a situation where an individual believes one thing and yet acts contrary to that belief there is conflict. This is called **'dissonance'.** He/she is motivated to lessen or to remove this 'dissonance'.

Festinger talks about **'cognitive elements'**, by which he means a piece of knowledge, a belief, or an opinion about either the environment or oneself. Other elements may include any behaviour of the individual. The elements may be:

(i)   **Consonant** ie. in harmony with each other

(ii)   **Dissonant** ie. in conflict with each other

(iii) **Irrelevant** ie. one element has no effect upon another

Examples
Figure 10 :

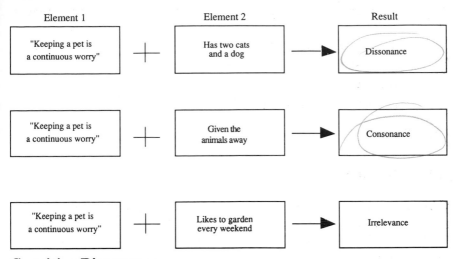

Cognitive Dissonance
(from Festinger 1957)

The magnitude of the dissonance produced by this conflict depends upon:

1 Importance to the person of the dissonant element.
2 The number of dissonant and consonant elements that exist at the same time. The greater the ratio of dissonant to consonant elements, the greater the dissonance felt.
3 The amount of cognitive overlap. The less the two events have in common the greater is the potential dissonance, e.g. a choice between fishing and going to the theatre would create greater dissonance than a choice between going to the cinema and going to the theatre.

Dissonance will go on increasing until it reaches a point where it is equal to the resistance to change of the least resistant of the elements. Then there is change and dissonance is reduced.

Post Decisional Dissonance

This is the term given to the feelings of unease that arise after a person has made a decision. The attitude held towards the chosen option will tend to become more favourable and those towards the unchosen option less favourable. For instance, attitudes about whether you are likely to win a bet, become much more favourable after the bet has been placed. People perceive they have made good decisions, after they have made them. The horse you back is seen as likely to run faster, simply because you have backed it.

There are a number of studies which have demonstrated this effect. **Aronson and Mills (1959)** divided female college students into three groups. Each group were told they would be listening to an exciting taped discussion about sex. The first group listened to the tape with no preliminaries, while the second had first to read a list of five sex related words - such as prostitute or virgin - to a male researcher. The third group had a more severe initiation. They had to read a dozen obscene four letter words and two very explicit sexual passages to a male researcher. Then instead of the expected discussion they had to listen to a boring report about animal sexual behaviour. Then they had to rate the value of the 'discussion'. The severer the initiation the more the discussion was valued. They had gone through the stress of a severe initiation and experienced cognitive dissonance when all they got was a boring talk about animal sexuality. Rather than feel upset they altered their attitude to the tape.

Other experiments on post-decisional dissonance include an interesting study by **Brehm (1966).** He aimed to test the hypotheses that
(i) Dissonance should be reduced by decreasing the attractiveness of the non-chosen options.
(ii) After the decision was taken, dissonance would be reduced if subjects were exposed to relevant information.
As payment for their participation in the experiment, the subjects (female) were allowed to take one of the items which they had previously been asked to rate for desirability.

Group A (high dissonance) had to choose between an item at the top of the ratings scale (very desirable) and one half to one and a half points lower on the eight point scale.

Group B (low dissonance) had to choose between a 'very desirable' item and one rated three points lower.

Subjects were then given research reports on the items rated. Half Group A and half Group B were given information on the items they had had to choose between. The other half had information on other items. Then they had to rate the items again.

Both halves of Group A and the half of Group B that had no information were shown to have increased the rated desirability of the chosen item and decreased the rating of the rejected item. Exposure to information after the decision did not reduce dissonance.

Two experiments into **forced compliance** illustrate other ways in which dissonance may alter attitudes.

Kelman (1953) asked school children to write an essay favouring comic book heroes, when he had previously found that they preferred other heroes.

Half were told that the whole class would get five tickets to a film as a reward. The other half were told that only five tickets per class would be awarded as prizes for the best essay.

Both groups tended to change their opinion of the heroes they wrote about. However, the second group changed more than the first. In the first condition all the children were to receive tickets, so there was some legitimate reason for writing counter- attitudinal essays. In the second condition, though, only the best were to be rewarded so that the dissonance was greater, and the attitude change was also greater.

Festinger and Carlsmith (1959) suggested that there was a relationship between the amount of pressure exerted to make a person comply and the degree of attitude change. They had two hypotheses

(i)   If forced compliance occurs then opinions will change to bring them into line with behaviour.

(ii) The stronger the pressure the weaker will be the tendency to change.

Male students were recruited to participate in a study of 'measures of performance'. Each subject performed two boring and repetitive tasks with the experimenter measuring performance. After the second task the experimenter explained that the purpose of the study was to compare task performance under two conditions:

1   The condition the subject had been in.

2   A condition where an assistant of the experimenter posing as some one who had just participated in the experiment told the next subject while he was waiting to participate in the study that the experiment was 'interesting and enjoyable ... fun ... intriguing ... exciting'. The object was to see how the subject's positive expectations of the experi ment influenced his performance.

Subjects were split into three groups, one control and two experimental.

1   **In the control condition** the subjects were directed to another room to answer questions in a survey allegedly unrelated to the experi ment.

2   **In the first experimental condition** the subjects were told that the experimenter's assistant was not available today and a fresh subject was already waiting to participate in the study. The subjects were asked to take on this assistant's role and tell the newcomer how 'inter- cating and enjoyable' the experimental tasks were. They were offered a fee of $1.

3   The **second experimental condition** was the same except that the fee offered was $20.

Subjects in the experimental conditions were then introduced to the new subject (in reality an assistant of the experimenter) and
told her that the tasks had been interesting and enjoyable. Then they were asked the same questions as the control group as part of an 'unrelated' survey. In the course of this survey they were asked 'Were the tasks interesting and enjoyable?' They answered this question by making a

rating on an eleven point scale.

Results showed that subjects in the first experimental condition rated the tasks more positively than the second, whose ratings were not significantly different from the control group. This supports the prediction by Festinger and Carlsmith on the basis of dissonance theory that under certain conditions the size of incentive is inversely related to the amount of attitude change.

Discussion of Festinger and Carlsmith study

Why is this finding consistent with dissonance theory?

(i) Two experimental groups engaged in **'counter-attitudinal behaviour'** in telling the waiting subjects that the tasks were interesting and enjoyable when they knew they were boring. This created dissonance. However, the payment is clearly consonant with the behaviour. The amount of the payment can be seen as equivalent to the importance of this consonant element. The payment of $20 has been seen as sufficient justification for having performed it. The $1 payment was insufficient justification and so the one dollar group experienced more cognitive dissonance which was reduced by changing their attitude to the experimental tasks.

Summary

The precise conditions under which this relationship between incentive and dissonance operates has been the subject of debate. This seems to have been shown most reliably when :

(a) Subjects feel they have voluntarily engaged in or committed themselves to the **'counter-attitudinal'** behaviour
   and
(b) Subjects believe that important consequences will arise as a result of performing the behaviour. **(Collins and Hoyt, 1972)**

The important elements seem to be :

(a) **Commitment :** If an individual does not feel committed to or bound by this decision there is no reason to experience dissonance. A publicly announced decision is more likely to arouse dissonance than a private one.

(b) **Volition or choice :** If an individual feels he has little or no choice in acting as he did then the amount of dissonance is minimised. 'Forced compliance' has tended to replace 'counter attitudinal' behaviour to describe the situation where there is pressure on us to act in a particular way.

Evaluation of dissonance theory

On the positive side, it can be said that dissonance theory :
1   has stimulated a great deal of discussion and research
2   can be applied to many situations and yet it is comparatively easy to design experimental tests of the theory
3   has a very broad application or range of convenience
4   has produced intriguing 'non-obvious' predictions borne out by experimental testing
5   cognitive dissonance researchers have produced ingenious and creative experimentation.

However, dissonance theory has been challenged by those who have argued that results could be explained by people's need to appear to others to be consistent. (**Tedeschi, Schlenker and Bonoma, 1971**) This view later became known as the **impression-management hypothesis.** (**Tedeschi, 1981: Malkis, Kalle and Tedeschi, 1982**)

For example, they argue that in the **Aronson and Mills** experiment described above subjects really thought the tape was boring but needed to appear consistent in the eyes of others and so said the tape was valuable. They did not wish to appear foolish to have gone through such a severe initiation in order to hear it. Their real attitudes had not changed, however. What has become known as the **'bogus pipeline'** procedure was employed to ascertain whether the attitudes reported were genuine or an attempt to enhance their image in the eyes of the researchers. Subjects were attached to a machine with an impressive display of flashing lights. They were told that this machine would reveal whether their answers represented their true opinions by monitoring their physiological responses. In order to establish the subject's confidence in the bogus pipeline, the first questions to be introduced in this procedure were some on which the subject's views had been subtly obtained some days before. The use of this procedure indicated that the subject's true attitudes often had not changed. (**Cialdini, Petty and Caccioppo, 1981**) Impression management must remain a possible explanation for the results obtained in experiments on cognitive dissonance. (**Cooper and Croyle, 1984**)

Self assessment questions

1   Describe what is meant by a **'cognitive element'** in relation to dissonance.

2   Cognitive elements are described as **'consonant', 'dissonant' or 'irrelevant'**; what is meant by these terms?

3   What does the magnitude of dissonance depend upon?

4   What is meant by **post-decisional dissonance?** Do the experiments conducted by Brehm, Kelman and Aronson and Mills adequately

49

5 What is the relationship between pressure to comply and the resulting dissonance?

6 How useful does dissonance theory seem to be as an explanation of attitude change?

7 What is meant by the **'impression-management hypothesis?'** Is it a viable alternative explanation for the results obtained in dissonance studies?

SECTION IV

ATTRIBUTION THEORY AND ATTITUDE CHANGE

(See also Chapter 2,)

Daryl Bem (1967, 1972)used attribution theory to attempt to explain the results of dissonance experiments such as that of Festinger and Carlsmith.

His objection to Festinger's theory was that it involved the operation of internal unobservable motives in all the processes of dissonance arousal and dissonance reduction.

It was argued that we explain our attitudes not through internal cues, or by introspection, but in terms of what we do. As was the case with Schachter's two-factor theory of emotion, the labelling of an internal state - an emotion in Schachter's case - or an attitude in Bem's - was partly internal and partly as a result of external cues. Bem contended that internal cues were often ambiguous and uninterpretable. In these cases, just as an observer infers states from observable behaviour so does the individual.

A man who is asked, "Do you like sailing?" and replies, "I suppose I do, I go out sailing every Sunday" is making use of his behaviour to provide an attitude statement. Applying these ideas to the dissonance experiments of **Festinger and Carlsmith (1959)** -
an outside observer hearing the subject making favourable statements about the experimental tasks he has performed to the next participant and knowing that payment was involved, would make inferences from this behaviour about the attitudes of the subject.

In the case of a small payment ($1) he might say to himself that he cannot be doing it for money - the money is too little - so the person's attitude must be consistent with this expressed statement. If the payment was large ($20) the observer might infer that that was the cause of his making the statement.

Bem argued that subjects viewed their own behaviour in the same light as an observer might. When asked about their attitudes they reviewed their behaviour and the context in which it occurred and came to the

50

their behaviour and the context in which it occurred and came to the conclusion either that the incentive was a sufficient cause of their behaviour or it was not.

West and Wickland (1980) came to the following conclusion about the dispute between Bem and the advocates of dissonance theory :-

"Dissonance theory applies readily when the person holds an extreme attitude or is in an extreme state, and then carries out behaviour contrary to that attitude. Self-perception theory generally provides the best account of attitude effects and other self description effects when the person does not have a strong attitude."

Self assessment questions

1   How does Bem use the attribution theories of Kelly and others to explain the results found in Festinger and Carlsmith's (1959) experiments?

2   How far do you think it is reasonable to transfer the inferences of **'locus of cause'** from perception of others to self-perception?

Further Reading

J. Richard Eiser, 1987, **Social Psychology Attitudes and Cognition,** Cambridge University Press.

Ben Reich and Christine Adcock, 1976, **Values, Attitudes and Behaviour Change,** London, Methuen (Essential Psychology Series)

"HEY! REMEMBER THE BAD OLD DAYS,
WHEN THEY MADE US WEAR SCHOOL
UNIFORM?"

Chapter 4

Norm Formation

At the end of this section students will be able to :

1 Identify what are meant by 'audience' and 'coaction'; and describe some of their effects.

2 Describe some studies of the effects of audience and coaction.

3 Describe what is meant by 'deindividuation' and its effects in relation to crowd behaviour.

4 State what is meant by 'bystander apathy' and describe the effects noted by Latané´ and Darley in the case of Kitty Genovese.

5 Put into their own words the meanings of the terms 'pluralistic ignorance' and 'diffusion of responsibility'.

6 Describe the role played by 'helping models' and also of information in changing behaviour in these circumstances.

7 Identify what are meant by normative, informational and ingratiational conformity

8 Distinguish between conformity and compliance.

9 Make some evaluation of the work of Sherif, Asch and Crutchfield on conformity.

10 Describe the experiments carried out by Stanley Milgram on obedience and make some evaluation of them.

11 Compare these experiments with others by Zimbardo and Hofling.

SECTION 1

SOCIAL FACILITATION

Social facilitation refers to the effect upon people of the presence or participation of others. It can refer to the effects when people work together or when they compete against one another, or simply to the effects upon an individual's behaviour of the presence of others, eg in a football crowd, or at the scene of an accident.

Audience and coaction

Triplett (1898) noticed that cyclists obtained better speeds when they raced against each other than against the clock. Then, in laboratory studies he instructed children to turn a fishing reel as fast as possible alone and also with others in the same room. The children, he found, worked faster in conditions of **'coaction'**

Later, **Dalshiel (1930)** noticed that coaction was not necessary, but that the mere presence of a passive spectator facilitated performance - ie. an **audience.**

Zajonc (1965, 1980) showed that the responses that improved were usually either

✓ (i)   highly practised,

or

(ii)   instinctive

Where the responses could easily be wrong, behaviour was often impaired by audience or by coaction, eg, in tests of multiplication, where there are many more wrong than right responses, the influence of another person either as co-actor or as observer was likely to be detrimental.

Some tests of social faciliation

In one study **(Zajonc, Heingartner and Herman, 1969)** cockroaches were able to run down a straight runway into a darkened goal box to escape a bright floodlight. They got to the goal box faster when they ran in pairs than when they ran alone. Then this test was repeated with an audience of four cockroaches, watching from behind a 'plexiglass' screen alongside the runway. This too increased their performance. But, of course, it has to be remembered that the reactions of cockroaches are not at all similar to those of humans!

Hunt and Hillery (1973) showed that with human subjects they would learn a maze faster with an audience provided it was a simple maze. A more complex maze was learnt more slowly in company.

✓ **Cottrell et al (1968)** found that it depended upon whether the individual felt he/she was being evaluated. When the audience was wearing a blindfold no audience effects at all are produced.

Markus (1978) made subjects change clothes with another subject and then change back. They were unobtrusively timed and it was found that when they did this alone, they took longer to put on someone else's outer clothes and shoes. However, when they were performing a well rehearsed task such as putting on their own clothes and shoes, they took longer when they had an audience.   This effect occurred even when the person in the room was not watching.

Crowd behaviour

Gustave le Bon (1895) claimed that the crowd is 'always intellectually inferior to the isolated individual ... mob man is fickle, credulous, and intolerant, showing the violence and ferocity of primitive beings'.

This led to the theory of **'deindividuation'** proposed first by **Festinger, Pepitone and Newcomb (1952)** and extended by **Zimbardo (1970) and Diener (1979, 1980).** These researchers have said that certain conditions present in groups lead to a state where personal identities are lost, merged into the group. (See Figure 11)

Figure 11 :

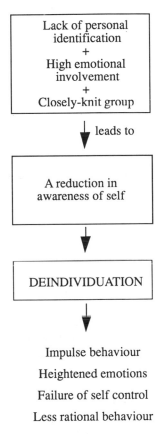

Impulse behaviour

Heightened emotions

Failure of self control

Less rational behaviour

The Process of Deindividuation

Some studies of deindividuation

Zimbardo (1970) required college women in groups of four to deliver electric shocks to another woman, who was supposedly in a learning experiment.

Half were deindividuated by making them feel anonymous. They wore laboratory coats and hoods and were spoken to always as a group, never by name.

The other half were not deindividuated. They remained in their own clothes and wore name tags. They were also introduced by name.

Both groups were asked to press a button to deliver shocks to the 'learners' when they made an error.

The deindividuated group were found to be prepared to deliver twice as much shock as the individuated group.

Diener (1976) had children engage in 'trick or treat' games at Halloween in identity-hiding costumes. Adults greeted them at the door and asked that each should take just one piece of candy. The adult then disappeared into the house and left the candy. Half the children had been asked their names, half had not. Those who remained anonymous stole more candy than those who did not.

Other factors influencing behaviour in later studies include the roles suggested by the outfits worn - Klu Klux Klan outfits or nurses uniforms - and also strongly held beliefs and the influence of a charismatic leader. An instance was the mass suicide at Jonestown, Guyana. Mob irresponsibility may also be due to lowered likelihood of being caught and punished.

Zimbardo's and Diener's studies could perhaps be criticised for doubtful ethics, particularly the use of children in experiments of this kind.

In Zimbardo's study, as in Milgram's (described in Section 3 of this chapter) subjects were deceived and put into the position of inflicting pain on others. Diener's study used children without their own or their parents' consent.

Bystander intervention

In 1964 Kitty Genovese was murdered outside her house in New York late at night. Because she resisted, the murder took more than half an hour. Although 40 neighbours heard her screams no-one called the police.

The incident led to investigations of **'bystander apathy'**. Deterrents to getting involved seemed to include physical danger, the possibility of a lengthy court appearance, unpreparedness for an emergency, and fear of making fools of themselves. **(Latané and Darley, 1970)**

Figure 12 illustrates the likely processes involved, resulting in what Latane and Darley call 'pluralistic ignorance' and inaction.

Figure 12 :

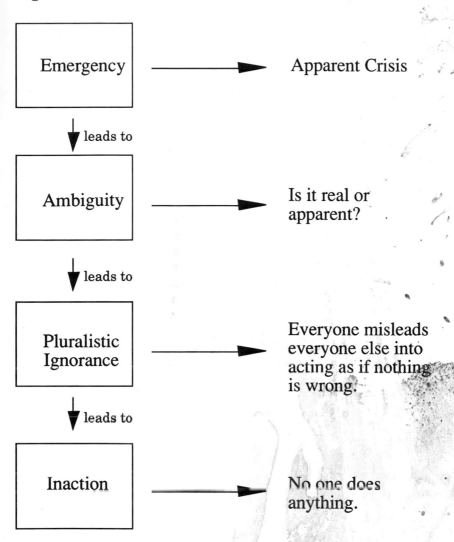

Pluralistic Ignorance (from Latané and Darley 1970)

Latané and Darley (1968) set up an experimental situation to investigate bystander apathy. Male college students were invited for interview. As they sat in a small waiting room, a stream of smoke began to pour through a wall vent. Some subjects were alone, some in groups of three. Experimenters observed them through a one-way window and waited six minutes.

Seventy-five per cent reported the smoke within two minutes when they were alone. In the groups of three fewer than 13 per cent reported the incident in the entire six minute period. They defined the occurrence to each other as a non-emergency.

Diffusion of responsibility

Pluralistic ignorance leads individuals to define the situation as a non-emergency, but a more important factor might be **'diffusion of responsibility'.** When individuals know others are present the burden of responsibility does not fall on them alone. Each thinks 'someone else will surely have done something by now'.

Tests of 'diffusion of responsibility'

Latané and Darley (1968) placed subjects in individual booths and told them they would take part in discussion about personal problems faced by college students. The discussion would be by intercom to avoid embarrassment. Each person would speak for two minutes, the microphone would be turned on only in the booth of the person speaking and the experimenter would not be listening. Actually the voices of all subjects were tape recordings.

In the first round, one of these participants mentioned he had problems with seizures. In the second round, this individual sounded as if he were starting a seizure and begged for help. Experimenters waited to see if subjects would leave the booth and report the emergency and how long it would take.

It is worth noting that

(i) The emergency was not ambiguous

(ii) The subject could not tell how the 'bystanders' in the other booths were reacting

(iii) The subject knew the experimenter could not hear the emergency

Some subjects were led to believe that the discussion group consisted of themselves only, others that there was a three person group, others a six person group.

A graph showing the results is contained in Figure 13.

58

Figure 13:

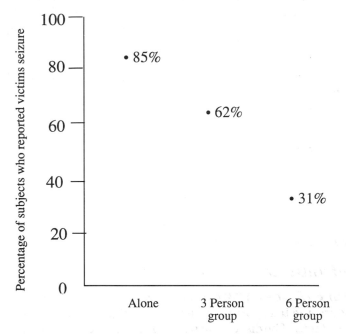

Results of Latané and Darley's (1968) study

Role of 'helping' models

It was suggested that when one person moved to help, others would follow. This possibility was examined by counting the number of people who stopped to help a woman whose car had had a flat tyre (test car). During some test periods another car with a flat tyre was stopped a quarter of a mile before the test car; a man had raised the car on a jack and was changing the wheel while a woman watched (model). Of 4,000 passing cars 93 stopped to help the woman alone in the test car, 35 stopped when there was no model and 58 when there was. **(Bryan and Test, 1967)**

Role of information

Would you be more likely to intervene in an emergency, now that you have read this section? Evidence from **Beaman et al (1978)** suggests that you would.

Self assessment questions

1   What is meant by 'coaction'? How does it affect people's behaviour?

2	What seemed to be the conditions under which the coactor effect facilitated performance in Zajonc's studies (1965, 1980)?

3	How was 'deindividuation' said to occur? Describe an experiment to test this effect.

4	What deterrents seemed to inhibit 'bystander intervention'?

5	What is meant by 'pluralistic ignorance' and 'diffusion of responsibility'? Describe some experiments to test these concepts.

6	What role do 'helping models' and 'information' play in altering people's behaviour?

7	In what ways would you regard some of the studies in this section as unethical?

SECTION II

CONFORMITY AND COMPLIANCE

Conformity : This amounts to the process where an individual adheres to the demands of a group, eg. a 'punk' may conform to the expectations of his/her group as much as the businessman with a dark suit, rolled umbrella and a bowler hat conforms to the norms of his own reference group, that is to **'significant others'**, ie. those other people who are important to him.

Mann (1969) says that **'the essence of conformity is yielding to group pressures'.**
He distinguished

1	**Normative conformity :** yielding to group pressure to accept the group norms under threat of rejection or promise of reward. This may be compliance - where he/she openly accepts the norms of the group but privately maintains his/her own view, or true conformity where he/she really believes as well as saying he/she does.

2	**Informational conformity :** where an individual is in an ambiguous or novel situation and is uncertain how to respond. So he/she looks to the statements or behaviour of others for guidance.

3	**Ingratiational conformity :** where a person agrees to impress or gain acceptance from a superior.

4	**Non-conformity :** This may amount to either (i) Independence of behaviour, or (ii) anti-conformity, which amounts to rebellion against group norms for its own sake.

Some studies of conformity and compliance

1	**Mustafa Sherif (1935)** studied conformity in the context of an optical illusion, the **'autokinetic effect'**. A small stationary light in a darkened room appears to move. Subjects tested individually estimated the movement of the light and a considerable variation was found in their judgements. When tested in groups subjects' estimates began to converge to a compromise estimate. Different groups produced different 'group unique' estimates.

A criticism might be that it was obvious they would conform since they had no other information and the light was not moving anyway. This might be said to represent informational conformity.

2 **Asch (1956)** tested subjects in groups of from six to nine seated in a straight line or round a table. Unknown to the one genuine subject all the rest were stooges of the experimenters. Subjects were given two cards such as in Figure 14

Figure 14:

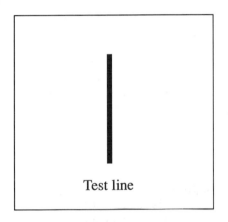

Test line

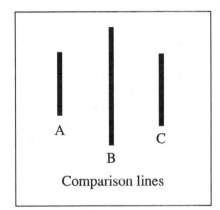

A

B

C

Comparison lines

Materials used in Asch's 1956 study

and asked to state which of the three comparison lines was the same as the test line. The subjects answered individually, the genuine subjects answering last. On certain predetermined **'critical'** trials the confederates gave the wrong answer. In these trials the genuine subject frequently 'conformed', ie. gave the same wrong answer as the stooges. Over fifty real subjects there was a mean of 3.84 conforming responses or 32 per cent. In control trials with individuals there were no errors.

Variations to the basic experiment highlighted various factors that may have determined the extent of conformity.

1 **Task difficulty :** where the comparison lines were more equal in length conformity increased.

2 **Majority size:** Asch systematically varied the number of confederates used to produce different sized majorities. Where there were two confederates the conformity was greater than with one and greater with three than two. Beyond three conformity remained the same.

3 **Unanimity:** Asch found that if even one of the confederates supported the genuine subject, conformity disappeared.

4 Where Ash arranged that one confederate answered correctly (along with genuine subject) for the first half of the critical trials, and then joined the majority, conformity was restored to almost the usual level (18.5 per cent).

5 **Status :** Where the confederates are regarded as of 'high status' the subject is even more likely to conform.

6 **Conditions of response :** Conformity decreased if subjects were not face-to-face with confederates.

Evaluation of Asch's research

1 Asch used the statistics of a mean conforming response where strictly, with a skewed distribution - as it was found to be - the median should have been used as the measure of central tendency. This would have brought the average level of conformity down from 32 per cent to 25 per cent.

2 In his trials Asch did not allow subjects to 'reserve judgement', as they might have been able to do in 'real life'. Nor could they ask advice or voice an opinion. The task also was rather a trivial one when related to 'real life'.

3 **Crutchfield (1954)** attempted a replication of Asch's research - using military men attending a three day assessment programme as subjects. Instead of confronting one another, subjects were in open cubicles in which were five adjacent electrical panels. They could not see their fellow subjects' panels. They had to respond to questions projected on to the wall by using lights on the panel A to E. Each subject found he responded first for a while then third, then fourth then second and finally last. He received feedback on other subjects' responses via the lights on his panel, but these were in fact connected to the experimenter's panel, not the other subjects. At any one time, each subject received the same information sent to the other four subjects, so that on any trial all five might be responding first, or all last.

The results were similar to Asch's but used a far wider range of materials, for instance attitudinal statements like, "I believe we are made better by the trials and hardships of life". In control conditions there was virtually no disagreement, but where it appeared that four had disagreed over 30 per cent also expressed disgreement. In response to the statement, "Free speech being a privilege rather than a right it is permissible to suspend free speech when a society feels threatened", 15 per cent agreed in control conditions 58 per cent in the conformity condition.

Crutchfield found that non-conformers showed more intellectual effectiveness, ego-strength, leadership ability and maturity in social relationships. They did not have the same feelings of inferiority, authoritarian tendencies or rigidity of thought as conformers. The non-conformer is efficient, expressive, aesthetic, active, natural, unpretentious and self-reliant. He is not submissive, narrow, inhibited and lacking in insight. Females are more conforming and also more conservative than men. However, adult women who had been to college were less conforming than their male counteparts.

Conclusion

Zajonc (1966) compares conformity to imitation which he says has important adaptive benefits. It means that each member of the group need not be treated individually. **Wheeler (1966)** refers to **behavioural contagion.** A person in a non-smoking compartment may desperately need a smoke but will not do so until he/she sees another traveller light up.

Self assessment questions

1 Distinguish between **normative conformity, informational conformity and ingratiational conformity.**

2 Which kind of conformity might the experiment of Sherif illustrate? Why?

3 What were the factors that determined the amount of conformity in Asch's study?

4 What were some of the criticisms of Asch's study?

5 What contributions did Crutchfield's study make to the study of conformity?

SECTION III

OBEDIENCE TO AUTHORITY

Obedience amounts to the willingness of people to acquiesce in the demands of another. This has been illustrated in real life by willingness of members of the Nazi party in Germany in the 1930s and 40s to commit atrocities just because they were told to.

A laboratory study carried out at Yale University by **Stanley Milgram (1963)** attempted to measure the level of subjects' obedience when instructed to inflict pain on others.

He used 40 male subjects who attended as a result of an advertisement and were paid $4.50 each to take part in an experiment on learning. They were introduced to Milgram in a white coat and the other 'subject' - actually an accomplice of Milgram's - an actor. The supposed purpose of the experiment was to be to evaluate the effect of 'punishment' in a paired-associate learning task. Where the learner made an incorrect response the "teacher" was to adminster an electric shock increasing from 15V to 450V.

The following table illustrates the number of subjects who gave in and refused to administer the shock at various voltages.

	Voltage	
Moderate shock	75v]	
	90v]	
	105v]	0
	120v]	
Very strong shock	195v]	
	210v]	
	225v]	0
	240v]	
Intense shock	255v	0
	270v	0
	285v	0
	300v	5
Extreme intensity shock	315v	4
	330v	2
	345v	1
	360v	1
Danger : severe shock	375v	0
	390v	0
	405v	0
	420v	0
	435v	0
	450v	26

As a result of interviews after the experiment and other criticisms Milgram carried out several variations of his basic design to test various possible reasons why obedience should have been as high as it was. He included proximity of the learner to the subject administering the shocks, proximity of Milgram himself, as experimenter, and status considerations.

1 **Proximity of the learner :** Three conditions were observed:

(a) In separate rooms (results above)

(b) 18" apart only so that teacher could see and hear the results of the shocks - 40 per cent still completed the experiment.

(c) 'Touch proximity' where the teacher had to force the learners hand down on the place to receive the shock. Still 30 per cent obeyed.

2 **Proximity of the experimenter :** Again three conditions

   (a) With the experimenter only a few feet away

   (b) With the experimenter present at first then left the room and gave subsequent instructions by phone

   (c) With the experimenter never present and instructions given by tape recorder. Obedience was almost three times greater in (a) than (c).

   (d) With the subject having a partner. Milgram ran one condition where the subjecthad two 'partners' who were also expected to shock the learner and who withdrew halfway through the series. 90 per cent of the subjects in this condition followed the partner's example and withdrew. (c.f.Studies of social facilitation in Section I of this chapter, pp. 58-60)

Milgram believed that the experimenter's position as a **'legitimate authority'** was an important factor which caused people to obey. In those conditions where the experimenter was absent and subjects were forced to take responsibility for their own actions, obedience was notably lower.

Baumrind (1964) criticised Milgram's studies on two grounds

(1) **Ethics of the whole thing.** Extreme trauma was experienced by subjects. Milgram justified this on two grounds.

   (a) He engaged in full explanations afterwards

   (b) The ends justified the means, ie the insights given into human nature justify the disturbances in subjects.

(2) **Questionable generality :** Could the findings be generalised into 'real life'? The unrepresentative nature of the samples - remember they were paid volunteers - also was called into question. Further it was felt that the prestigious nature of the institution (Yale University) and the authority of the experimenter also affected the results.

To counter this last criticism he repeated his experiment in a 'run-down office building' outside the University. 50 per cent of the men obeyed until the end in these conditions also.

    Other experiments into this area of obedience tend on the whole to add credence to Milgram's findings. Direct replications by **Mantell (1971)** in Germany found even greater obedience (85%). In Jordan **(Shanat and Yahya)** found 80% and studies by **Ancona and Pareysin** in Italy (1968) and **Kilham and Mann (1974)** in Australia also found high levels of obedience.

    A much more realistic study done by **Hofling et al (1966)** also supports Milgram's findings.

Nurses were instructed by a 'doctor' - in fact a confederate of the experimenter - by telephone to give 20 mg. of the drug Astrofen to his patient, Mr. Jones. He would come to see Mr. Jones in 10 minutes and would sign for the drug then. If she agreed the nurse would be breaking three rules:

(1) The maximum dose prescribed for this drug was 10 mg.

(2) Written authority was required before a drug was administered

(3) A nurse should check the genuineness of the 'doctor'.

21 out of 22 nurses complied with the telephoned request.

Zimbardo et al (1973) carried out an experiment which relates to this question. It also looks into the issue of **'social power'** and the way it is built into the roles we adopt. They selected 25, after extensive tests, out of the 100 applicants who came forward to volunteer for this study. The fee offered was generous. Subjects were to be either 'prisoners' or 'prison guards' in a simulated prison.

They were assigned to either role at the toss of a coin. At the beginning of the experiment the prisoners were arrested, charged with felony and made to go through all the degrading procedures which follow upon this: strip-searching, de-lousing, being given a prison uniform with a number front and back, and even a manacle on one ankle.

The 'guards' had military style uniforms, reflective sunglasses to prevent eye contact, clubs, whistles, handcuffs and keys. They shouted orders, pushed the prisoners about. Any abuse was allowed short of physical violence. While the 'prisoners' were locked up around the clock the 'guards' worked eight hour shifts.

In a short time a perverted relationship developed between 'prisoners' and 'guards'. The guards stepped up their aggression, the prisoners became more passive. Within 36 hours one prisoner had broken down, begging to be released, developed depressive symptoms and had to be released. Other prisoners developed similar 'stress' symptoms and the whole experiment - due to run for a fortnight - had to be called off after six days.

As with Milgram's work, Zimbardo has come under criticism for the ethics involved. Did the ends of this research - the uncovering of hidden propensities for evil in normal human beings - justify the "deceiving, humiliation and maltreatment of subjects" (Savin, 1973)?

Self - assessment questions

1 How did Milgram obtain his subjects for this experiment? Was this a representative sample? If not, why not?

2 What were the factors which caused the subjects to obey?

3 Outline some of the criticisms made of the experiment.

4 Compare Milgram's work with that of Zimbardo and Hofling.

"BEFORE YOU EXERCISE YOUR LEGITIMATE POWER TO USE COERCIVE POWER, SIR, I HAPPEN TO HAVE THIS INFORMATIONAL POWER..."

Chapter 5

Co-operation or Conflict

At the end of this chapter you should be able to :

1   Describe some of the circumstances in which people will co- operate and help one another.

2   Describe and comment critically upon some of the experiments conducted to investigate **co-operation.**

3   Comment upon the use of experimental games such as the **'Trucking Game'** and the **'Prisoner's Dilemma'** in relation to their ability to explain **co-operation and conflict.**

4   Identify some of the factors which have been cited as contributing to the build up of **aggression.**

5   Make some assessment of the effect of TV violence on aggressive behaviour.

6   Identify some of the ways in which the likelihood of violence may be reduced.

Introduction

In this chapter we shall attempt to discuss some of the evidence that suggests, either that people are co-operative and will help each other or else that they are naturally aggressive and competitive. The study of aggression has a long history and includes study of aggressive behaviour not only among humans but among animals. Altruism and co-operation among animals will be the subject of a section in a later volume.

SECTION I

ALTRUISM AND HELPING

Co-operation may be defined as doing something with another person for the attainment of mutual benefits. However, there are cases where individuals unilaterally 'do good' to another person, without any expectations of benefit sometimes at considerable cost to himself. This has been called **'altruism' or pro- social behaviour.**

Richard Dawkins (1976) in his book **'The Selfish Gene'** looked at the way in which animals devote themselves to the welfare and therefore to the survival of other members of their species. There is also a great deal of research into the way humans may avoid the responsibility of giving assistance to strangers in case of need - **(see Rosenthal's (1964)** account of the murder of Kitty Genovese or the simulated bystander apathy studies of Latané and Darley in Section I of Chapter 4).

An experiment by **Ross and Braband (1973)** suggests help may depend upon the reaction of others to the situation. Subjects were required to work on a card-sorting task - either alone or in the presence of either a normally- sighted or supposedly blind confederate. After the experimenter left the room one of two emergencies occurred :

(i) The sound of a workman hurting himself and screaming.

(ii) The sound of glass crashing followed by smoke pouring into the experimental room from another part of the laboratory. This had supposedly been taken over by the chemistry department who had put a notice on the door 'Dangerous Work in Progress'. Neither emergency produced any reaction from the confederate.

In the case of the **'scream'** emergency 64 per cent of subjects when tested alone left their card-sorting task within five minutes to go and investigate. When paired with a confederate 28 per cent reacted if he was blind, 35 per cent if he was sighted. In the **'smoke'** condition 50 per cent reacted when alone, 64 per cent when paired with a blind confederate and 14 per cent paired with a sighted one. In the 'smoke' condition where the signs of emergency were mainly visual, the subject could not infer from the inactivity of the 'blind' confederate what his response should be and so reacted as though he was alone. Where the emergency was an audible one, the unresponsiveness of the 'blind' confederate inhibited reaction equally with the one who was sighted.

Ambiguity seems also to be a factor. **Clark and Word (1972)** found that all subjects interviewed went to help when a maintenance man was heard to fall and cry out in agony, regardless of the size of the group, while if only the fall was heard the percentage helping dropped to 30 per cent. The ambiguity about what the emergency was, was greater, and there was also ambiguity about what ought to be done.

Darley and Latané (1970) had passers-by approached and asked for a minimal amount of money (10 cents). 34 per cent handed over the money. When the request was explained by the actor saying that he needed to make a telephone call 64 per cent responded. When the reason given was that his wallet had been stolen the proportion rose to 70 per cent.

Dorris (1972) approached a number of coin dealers with some rare coins which he said he had inherited. The average initial offer he received was $8.72 for coins worth $12, when no further explanation was given. When he said he needed money to buy text books for his examination the average offer rose to $13.63.

There seems also to be a strong inclination to weigh up the deserts of the person asking for help, and whether the individual would be justified in withholding it. There is a strong temptation to see others as deserving the misfortunes that befall them.

When four students were shot dead by Ohio National Guardsmen at Kent State University, a high school teacher asserted that they deserved to die. "Anyone who appears on the streets of a city like Kent, with long hair, dirty clothes and bare-footed deserves to be shot". **(Michener, 1971)**

The criterion for what is just or deserving seems often to rest with what others would do in the same circumstances. A person likes to feel he is 'doing his bit' to help. The spontaneous reaction to the 'Band Aid' appeal for famine in Africa illustrates this.

However, provided that the rules of fair play are observed an individual will not be criticised for capitalising on any extra bit of 'luck' that comes his way. **Lerner and Lichtman (1968)** refer to norms of justified self-interest, in explaining the results of the study they conducted.

Subjects were female students. They were told that they were to participate in a learning experiment in one of three conditions :

(a) The **'shock'** condition, where they were to receive electric shocks, or

(b) The **control** condition where they received no shocks.

They could choose which condition they participated in. Their partners would take the other condition. They either :

(i) were given to understand that they were given this choice on an entirely random basis, or

(ii) they were told that their partner had asked the experimenter to pass on the message that they were really scared about the 'shocks' and would prefer to be in the control condition, or

(iii) they were told that their partner had initially been the one to be given the choice and had said "they preferred to let you decide".

In the first condition nine per cent chose the shock condition for themselves whereas in the second condition 72 per cent chose the shock for themselves. In the third condition 88 per cent put themselves in the shock condition.

These results do not support the notion that human beings are fundamentally self-centred, amoral and cynical in their social interactions.

They seem to be scrupulously concerned with what is 'fair'. This norm of fairness allows them to act in their own self-interest if the situation is perceived to be one of fair competition, even to the detriment of others.

Experimental games

Investigations of co-operation and competition have sometimes taken the form of games.

Examples are :

(i) The 'TRUCKING GAME developed by **Deutsch and Krauss (1960, 1962)**.

In this there are two players each of whom is supposed to be operating a trucking firm named 'Acme' and 'Bolt'. Each gets paid a fixed sum, minus a variable cost dependent upon the length of time taken for each load of merchandise to be delivered to its destination. Each has two possible routes :

(i) A short main route involving a small section of one way road

(ii) A longer route which would involve a loss of premium

There is a danger that both players will attempt to use the one- way road at the same time and meet head on, then one player would have to back out, unless there was to be a deadlock and mutual loss.

Deutsch and Krauss also manipulated various 'threats' to the emergence of co-operation by giving one or other or both players control of gates at either end of the one-way road. Figure 15 illustrates the road map for the trucking game.

Figure 15:

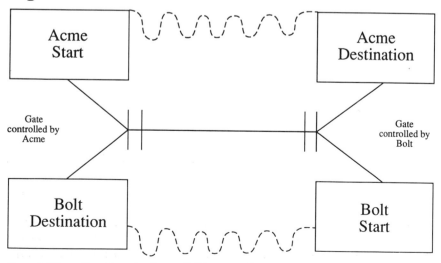

Road Map for Deutsch and Krauss Trucking Game (1962)

(ii) **PRISONER'S DILEMMA**

An imaginary situation was set up in which two accomplices are awaiting trial.

They have the option either :

    (i) of informing on the other

    (ii) not saying anything

The outcomes are seen to be different in each case. They depend on each player's decision and that of his opponent.

Each person in the two-person laboratory game has a possible two choices, co-operation (C) or defection (D). See Figure 16.

Figure16:

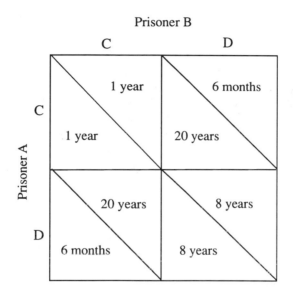

The Prisoners Dilemma
(from Luce and Raiffa 1957)

The prisoners cannot plan their strategy as they are not able to communicate. They can only guess at what the other will do. If they could both be certain that the other would co-operate (not confess) that would be the best strategy.

   This kind of dilemma becomes fairly common in situations where the outcomes are determined not only by our actions but also by those of others. For example, in a panic situation - such as a fire in a theatre - an individual has two options :

1 to rush for the exit,

2 to proceed calmly.

The best outcome, it has been shown, for both parties, is to co-operate with each other. However, this seems to be comparatively rare, as the urge to compete leads to one or other breaking ranks.

Attempts to identify factors which might make players less competitive and more co-operative have focused upon the following:

1 **The other player's strategy :** Often in laboratory situations the other player is simulated or is a confederate playing a pre-determined game. These strategies might be 100 per cent co-operation (C) or, alternatively, 100 per cent competition (D).

One hundred per cent co-operation produces more co-operation in return while 100 per cent competition tends to force the other player to compete in self-defence.

Another pre-determined strategy is Tit for Tat (TFT). The confederate chooses, on each trial, the response chosen by the subject on the previous trial.

This has the result of rewarding the subject for co-operation and punishing him for defection.

2 **The nature of the rewards :** The actual pay-offs in a laboratory are often merely in the form of 'points' which have no significance other than in the game. Since mutual co-operation is the means whereby the highest joint profit can be achieved, by giving only negligible rewards one may effectively be removing any incentive for co-operation.

Playing for real money seems to result in greater co-operation (McClintock and McNeel, 1966).

3 **Lack of opportunity to communicate :** This seems to be the cause of the low levels of co-operation.

Voissem and Sistrunk (1971) found that subjects who could pass notes of a standard form expressing their intentions and expectations before each trial of a 100 trial game became progressively more co-operative as compared to a no communication group, who became more competitive as the game progessed.

Wichman (1970) had women play 78 trials of PD under :

1 an isolated condition (where they could neither hear nor see each other)

2 a condition where they could hear but not see

3 a condition where they could see but not hear

4 a condition where they could both see and hear

The median levels of co-operation over the first 70 trials in each condition were

1   40.7 per cent
2   47.7 per cent
3   72.1 per cent
4   87.0 per cent

The more freely and naturally subjects can communicate the more they co-operate.

Self- assessment questions

1   Describe Ross and Braband's (1973) experiment into helping behaviour. What were its main conclusions?

2   What were the factors that seemed to influence **'helping behaviour'?**

3   Describe Deutsch and Krauss's **'trucking game'.** What variables did they manipulate to discover factors which influence the level of co-operation?

4   What factors seem to influence the level of co-operation in the **'games'** **setting** (Prisoner's Dilemma and Trucking Game).

SECTION II

AGGRESSION AND VIOLENCE

Introduction

The study of aggression and violence has a long history and includes not only aggression amongst humans but also animal aggression. In this section the intention is to investigate only aggressive behaviour where it relates to groups of human subjects, either children or adults.

In psychology there has been some inconsistency in accounts of what is meant by aggression. In general it might be defined as verbal or non-verbal behaviour intended to cause harm to people or property.

Frustration - aggression hypothesis (Dollard et al 1939)

Basic suggestions were made that :

1   Frustration always leads to some form of aggression.
2   Aggression is always the result of frustration.

There are problems with this hypothesis

1   It is now clear that frustrated individuals do not always turn to

aggression. Responses to being obstructed in attempts to reach a goal may range from resignation to attempts to get at the source of the obstruction and remove it. In many cases frustration results in depression rather than overt aggression. **(Bandura, 1973)**

2   It is clear also that all aggression does not result from frustration in every case. A boxer might be aggressive because it is part of his job. An assassin might act aggressively for money. The hypothesis has therefore been modified to state that frustration sometimes results in aggression. **(Berkowitz, 1978)** But this, of course, does not say very much about aggression. It is evident though that frustration needs to be quite strong to produce aggression, and also unexpected. **(Baron, 1977: Morchel, 1974)**

Conditions which elicit aggression

1   **Direct provocation from others :**
Physical abuse or verbal taunts may act as powerful elicitors of aggression, which, once it begins, has a way of rapidly escalating. **(Goldstein et al, 1975)**

Laboratory studies such as those of **Kimble, Fitz and Onorad (1977) and Dengerink, Schnedler and Covey (1978)** show that 'turning the other cheek' is not a usual response to aggression. Those who receive attacks normally respond in kind. Sometimes aggression is a response merely to learned intentions on the part of the other person. **(Greenwell and Dengerink, 1973: Dyek and Rule, 1978).** Reciprocity seems to play a large part.

2   **Exposure to aggressive models :**
Bandura (1977) suggested that people become aggressive because they have learned by experience, observation and imitation that it pays. Frustration does not innately lead to aggression but will do so when it has been learnt that it is rewarding. Humans learn this not only by being reinforced when they act aggressively, but by observing others being so reinforced and then imitating them.

Equally we learn that other responses are also rewarding, such as

-    withdrawal from the situation

-    attempting even harder to solve it rationally

-    rationalising what has happened

-    anaesthetising oneself with alcohol or drugs

Bandura and Walters (1973) showed that nursery school children became more aggressive towards 'Bobo' dolls if they had previously seen a live or filmed model treating the dolls violently. And these effects were strengthened when the imitator was reinforced for his behaviour.

Parke et al (1977) showed similar effects where subjects were exposed to either violent or non-violent TV programmes for several weeks. They seemed uniformly to be more willing to engage in aggression when they had been watching violence than when they had been watching non-violent films.

The effects mentioned above arise through :

1 **observable learning :** this equips them with new techniques for harming others

2 **desensitization to aggression :** after watching many violent programmes they are no longer emotionally upset or aroused by such behaviour.(**Thomas et al, 1977**)

3 **a reduction in restraints against violence :** "If adult characters in TV shows can behave like this, so can I", is the reasoning.

Figure 17:

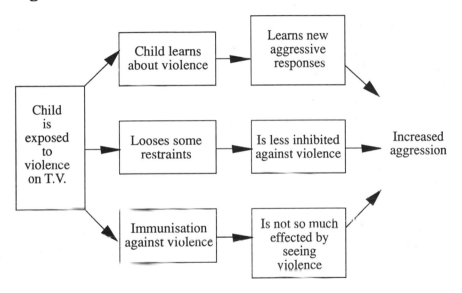

Effects of T.V violence

In one study by **Eron et al (1972)** with American boys it was shown that the amount of TV violence watched at the age of nine was a good predictor of aggressiveness ten years later.

Gerbner and Gross (1976) showed that 'heavy' watchers of TV were more distrustful, over-estimated the risk of criminal violence and bought more locks, dogs and guns to protect themselves, than those who watched less TV violence.

It is possible that some other factor unknown to the investigator may be responsible for these findings. For example, individuals who display aggressive behaviour may have a natural pre-disposition to behave aggressively, which in turn may motivate them to watch more TV violence.

The opposite views are that watching violence is cathartic and releases pent up aggression. These views stem from Freud and some of the ethologists but do not seem to be borne out by other studies. Adults, when given repeated opportunities to adminster shocks to an unretaliating victim become more, not less, punitive **(Buss, 1966)**. Angry subjects in another study by **Loew (1967)** became more vicious with repeated attacks.

3   Other determinants of aggression

(i) **Heat, crowding and noise :** Environmental conditions such as heat, crowding and noise have all been found to increase aggression. **(Donnerstein and Wilson, 1976a; Baron, 1978a)**

(ii) **Heightened arousal :** Whatever its source heightened arousal can enhance aggression **(Zillman, 1979)**. This is especially so in cases where we are concerned about the source of our arousal and tend to label it 'irritation' or anger.

(iii) **Drugs :** Alcohol in small amounts seem to put people in a 'happy' state of mind and reduce overt aggression **(Taylor et al, 1976)**. Larger amounts reduce inhibitions and increase the likelihood of aggression.

4   Genetic determinants

It has been shown that men who possess an extra Y chromosome instead of the more normal XY pattern are far more common in the prison population than in the general population. **(Jacobs, Brunton and Melville, 1965)**. While only one newborn baby boy in a thousand is XYY 15 prisoners out of 1000 fall into this category. It was suggested that XYY individuals are genetically programmed to be more violent. While some research **(Bandura, 1973)** has supported this, a large scale study by **Witkin et al (1976)** found no evidence of it. The researchers tested 4591 Danish men to find their chromosome pattern. 4139 were XY, 12 were XYY and 16 were XXY. Information about these people was collected from public records, regarding height, intelligence, criminal records, etc.

Results showed

1   No evidence whatsoever that XYY individuals were more aggressive.

2   Some evidence was found for the suggestion that XYYs were not as bright as average and so might be likely to be caught and convicted of crime.

Prevention and control of aggression

Punishment :

1 The present state of research suggests that punishment produces only a temporary suppression of punished actions.

2 Those who are punished often view it as an unjustified attack and so a provocation for further aggression.

3 Those who administer punishment may serve as aggressive models for those who receive it.

Catharsis hypothesis : The idea of 'getting it out of your system'.

It has been suggested that providing angry people with the chance to 'blow off steam' would :

1 lower their arousal level

2 reduce their tendency to engage in harmful acts of aggression.

Hokauson (1970) has found that angry persons experienced reductions of annoyance or arousal when permitted to engage in tension-releasing activity.

Evidence for the second part of the hypothesis, though, is not clear. While some studies found evidence for catharsis **(Fromkin, Goldstein and Brock, 1977),** others found the opposite. Aggression actually increased. **(Geen, Stoner and Shope, 1975)**

Conclusions seem to be that :

1 Catharsis may occur and sometimes may reduce overt aggression, but only under quite specific conditions.

2 When it does occur it is usually short-lived.

Incompatible responses

No one is capable of engaging in two incompatible responses at once. The reduction of aggression may come through the introduction of responses incompatible with anger The responses that have been studied are 'humour' and 'mild sexual arousal'.

(i) **Humour: Mueller and Donnerstein (1977)** showed that in almost all cases angry persons were made less angry by exposure to humorous material. Subjects were first made angry by an accomplice of the experimenter and then shown either humorous cartoons or neutral material (eg. pictures of scenery). They they were permitted to act aggressively towards the person who provoked them. Those exposed to humour showed much lower levels of aggression than those exposed to the neutral material.

(ii) **Mild sexual arousal :** exposure to mild forms of erotica have been shown to be effective in reducing overt aggression. **(Baron, 1974, 1979; Fode, 1977)** Stronger sexual arousal, however, does not seem to have the same effect.

Self - assessment questions

1 Does the **'frustration-aggression'** hypothesis of Dollard appear to be supported? What are its faults?

2 What conditions seem to elicit aggressive behaviour?

3 What is the evidence that exposure to violence on TV is likely to produce more aggressive behaviour?

4 Does there seem to be any evidence that violence may be genetic in origin?

5 What ways have been investigated to control or reduce aggressive behaviour? How successful have they been?

Further Reading :

Baron, R.A., Byrne, D., and Kantowitz, B.H., **Psychology: Understanding Behaviour,** 2nd ed., Holt Saunders, 1980, Ch. 13.

Gahagan, J., **Interpersonal and Group Behaviour,** Methuen, 1975, Ch. 7.

Richard Eiser in Tajfel H. and Fraser C., (eds) Introducing **Social Psychology,** Penguin, 1978, Ch. 6.

"IT'S REALLY HOMEWORK — I NEED TO PREPARE MYSELF FOR THE PUNCH-UP IN THE PLAYGROUND TOMORROW."

Chapter 6

Working in Groups

SECTION I

SMALL GROUP STRUCTURE

At the end of this chapter students will be able to :

1 Identify the necessary criteria for a 'group'.
2 Identify kinds of group structures that have been studied.
3 Describe and comment on Leavitt's analysis of the effects of different communication structures.
4 Describe what is meant by **'power structure'** and the kinds of power that may exist in a group.
5 Identify and describe the five approaches that have been made to the study of leadership.
6 Make some evaluation of the **'contingency model'** of leadership effectiveness produced by Fiedler.
7 Describe and evaluate the work of Lewin Lippitt and White into styles of leadership.

Power and influence

Two's a dyad, three's a small group. Essentially the interactions that occur when there are more than two people together are different from those where there are just two. As far as the largest size of a 'small group' is concerned perhaps the proposal of Bales (1950) is relevant :

"Provided that each member receives some impression or perception of each other member distinct enough .. that he can give some reaction to each of the others as an individual person then a collection of people can be termed a small group."

The criteria for a small group seem to include the following :

1 **Interaction** sustained over a sufficient period of time.

2   **Perception** of the existence of a group and of themselves as members of it.

3   **Norm formation:** the members of the group tend to act and to expect other members to act in standard ways, and members who disregard the norms lay themselves open to disapproval and possible sanctions by group members.

4   **Roles** will develop within the group around certain positions within the group - chairman, food-preparer etc. - so that these roles develop their own norms.

5   **Affective relations:** some members will be liked or disliked so that a pattern of affective relationships will develop.

6   **Shared goals:** a group will develop shared goals. Even where these purposes are externally set they will tend to be interpreted and re-interpreted according to its own norms. Almost certainly additional goals will be generated by the group itself.

These criteria should be sufficient to enable us to decide when people waiting in a queue for a bus cease to be a set of people and become a group. While there are many kinds of small groups the vast majority of those that have been studied by social psychologists have been **'laboratory groups'** - ie groups brought together for the specific purposes of study. **McGrath and Altman (1966)** reported that out of well over 2000 reports of small group studies 55 per cent had been conducted in the laboratory, a further 30 per cent had more laboratory than field elements and only five per cent were genuine studies carried out in natural settings.

Group structures

Within a group it is possible to identify several independently existing structures which include the **affective structure,** the **communication structure** and the **power structure** of the group.

1   Affective structure

This has largely been studied by means of sociometry. Group members are asked to select those of the group they most like. The resulting choices are represented on a sociogram - a schematic diagram showing the number and direction of choices. This is particularly useful with classroom sized groups. At a glance you can identify those members of the group that are popular and those who are isolates and also the presence of any incipient subgroups (see Attraction, Chapter II, Section 3, p.)

Example : A hypothetical six person group might have choices as represented in Figure 18.

Figure 18:

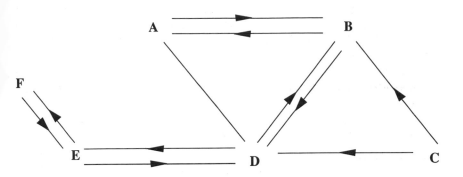

Sociometry : A hypothetical six person group

D is clearly popular.

C is a bit of an isolate.

There are also subgroups A and B and E and F with D having links with both.

2   **Communication structure**

This is either laid down by some **external influence** - as with a committee where the chairman and other officers are appointed - or else **emerges naturally** from the group as it works.

Bavelas (1950) described a laboratory situation where subjects were in individual booths. There were slots in the walls by means of which they could pass written messages. By opening or closing different slots different networks could be created.

Leavitt (1951) used some of these networks to investigate the relative efficiency of five person groups with different structures in solving simple identification problems - eg which symbols were common to all the cards distributed to group members. More centralised networks, based on a leader, were found to be more efficient than less centralised. (The wheel, for example, rather than the circle). See Figure 19.

Figure 19:

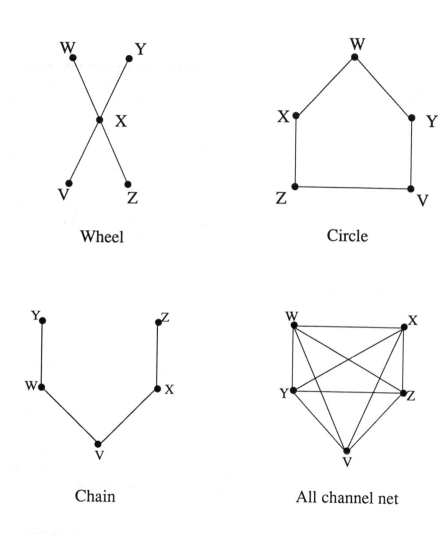

Wheel

Circle

Chain

All channel net

Communication Networks (from Leavitt 1951)

While Leavitt showed that this was the case for simple tasks **Shaw (1954)** found the opposite to be the case when the task was complex. In the latter situation, with an all channel net where each member can communicate with every other member, more opportunity is given for free exchange of information.

Formal and informal networks

Mulder (1960) showed that there could exist side by side the formal, imposed network and informal individual decision making structure emerging from it. He calculated for each group a **'decision centrality index'**, the discrepancy between the most active and the next most active sender of decision taking messages.

The determinants of efficiency seemed to be :

(i)   the topological structure of the communication net

(ii)   the centralisation of decision-taking

More centralised 'wheels' were found to be most efficient, followed by less centralised 'wheels'. The least efficient were the less centralised circles. It is not clear whether these studies, conducted in artificial situations, have 'real world' validity.

3   Power structure.

It is possible to consider the power structure of a group in terms of :

(i)   The individuals in a group

(ii)   The positions individuals hold in a group

(iii)   Some mixture of the above

Collins and Raven (1969) identify **'social power'** as "the potential influence of some influencing agent O over some person P. Influence is defined as a change in cognition, attitude, behaviour or emotion of P which can be attributed to O'.

They identify six different types of power :

(i)   **Reward power**   - P sees that O has power to reward him.

(ii)   **Coercive power**   - P sees that O has power to punish him.

(iii)   **Referent power**   - P wishes to identify with O.

(iv)   **Expert power**   - P attributes greater knowledge to O.

(v)   **Legitimate power**   - P accepts norms that O should have.

(vi)   **Informational power**- based upon information which is independent of the nature of the source.

In each of (i) - (v) the power is dependent upon some perceived attribute in O.

In (vi) information is power independent of the source

Examples :

(a) Your boss has **reward power** over you - he can promote you.

(b) He also has **coercive power** - he can sack you.

(c) A pop star exercises **referent power** over his fans who want to identify with him.

(d) A teacher - one hopes - has **expert power** over his pupils, ie he has knowledge, expertise and skills which they want.

(e) The head of a school has **legitimate power** over his staff and pupils - he has been duly appointed and they accept the norm of obedience to legitimate authority.

(f) If, however, a member of the staff knew that the head had been embezzling the funds, that **information** would give him **power** over the head. That would be independent of any attribute the head might have.

Collins and Raven (1969) argue that group behaviour will, to some extent, be determined by the type of power that is exercised. However, these power structures are not independent of one another but interdependent.

Cartwright and Zander (1968) suggests that separate types of structure may not in fact operate independently.

4 Role structure

This is very closely related to the communication structure. **Bales (1970) Interaction Process Analysis (IPA)** used trained observers who coded each behavioural act as it occurred in a group according to twelve categories. He assembled small ad hoc groups in a laboratory and scored their verbal interactions by means of IPA.

There emerged two distinct types of leader - what could be described as a task leader who tended to be oriented towards achieving the group's goals, and a socio-emotional leader who was warm, friendly and supportive towards the group members, and whose function appeared to be to keep up this morale.

Bales catagories

**Emotional area A :
questions**

[1   Shows solidarity, raises others
[morale, gives help or reward.
[
[2   Shows tension release, jokes,
[laughs, shows satisfaction.
[
[3   Agrees, shows passive acceptance,
      understands, concurs, complies.

**Task area :
attempted
answer**

[4   Gives suggestion, direction,
[implying autonomy for others.
[
[5   Gives opinion, evaluation,
[analysis, expresses feelings
[wishes.
[
[6   Gives orientation, information,
[repeats, clarifies, confirms.

**Task area :
positive
reactions**

[7   Asks for orientation, information,
[repetition, confirmation.
[
[8   Asks for opinion, evaluation,
[analysis, expression of feeling.
[
[9   Asks for suggestion, direction,
[possible ways of action.

**Emotional area D :
negative
reactions**

[10 Disagrees, shows passive
[rejection, formality, withholds
[help.
[
[11 Shows tension, asks for help
[withdraws out of field.
[
[12 Shows antagonism, deflates
[another's status, defends or
[asserts self

Figure 20: System of categories used in IPA (Bales 1970)

Bales and Slater (1955) found that of the most talkative members of a group there seemed to be two distinct types of 'leader'.

1 The one who scored most highly in the 'attempted answers' category (B) tended to be seen as the group leader. They were most concerned with achieving the group's goals.

2 The one who scored most highly in the 'positive sections' category (C). His role seemed to be the maintenance of good interpersonal relations with the group.

Self assessment questions

1 What are the criteria for a group?

   ie when is a group not a group?

2 What kinds of small group have been studied? What comments might be made about the artificiality of these studies?

3 What means have been used to investigate the affective structure of groups? Comment on the use of sociograms.

4 What kinds of communication structure did Leavitt and others investigate?

5 What kinds of power have been identified?

SECTION II

LEADERSHIP

Leadership might be defined as any behaviour that moves the group towards the attainment of its goals. It is not material whether this is behaviour that emanated from one person, two or three people, or whether it is evenly spread through the group.

Hollander and Julian (1969) reviewing the research on leadership say "The history of leadership research is a fitful one. Certainly as much, and perhaps more than other social phenomena, conceptions and inquiry about leadership have shifted about."

There seem to be five approaches that have been made to the subject:

(i) A study of personality characteristics of leaders

This has tended to concentrate upon an account of the personalities of those identified by common consent as leaders. While this was not the most fruitful of approaches there are some generalisations that emerged

1 Leaders are generally **intelligent** - they score higher than the average of other group members on intelligence, relevant knowledge and verbal facility.

2   They are generally **sociable:** measures of social participation, co-operation and popularity showed them to be higher than average.

3   They are also highly **motivated, persistent** and possessed of a high degree of **initiative.**

(ii) Situational factors

This approach attempted to identify any cross-situational characteristics of leadership that might exist. To what extent were leaders consistent or inconsistent across a variety of situations? However, this approach has been shown to be very fragile.

(iii) Leadership functions

Various experiments have isolated functions of leadership in quite different situations, ranging from studies of bomber-crews, to undergraduates in laboratory groups: These behaviours appear to resolve themselves into the two main categories we have already discussed in Section 1, and which were identified by Bales (1970), that is **'task leadership'** and **'socio-emotional leadership'.**

(iv) Leadership roles

This approach suggests that there are certain stable and well-defined roles which can be identified within a group as leadership roles. Were the individuals who occupied these roles to leave, the position would remain and the leadership structure would be relatively unchanged, with different people performing different functions.

Bales analysis which is described in Section I seems to fulfil these requirements. This suggested - certainly as far as laboratory studies were concerned - that there would ordinarily be two people in a group exercising leadership of the two different kinds. **Verba (1960),** however, used 'real' groups as opposed to laboratory ones and showed that the task leader often had organisational or institutional legitimacy.

If a Head of Department is seen to be providing the legitimate goals which his function demands then not only are his subordinates better disposed towards him, but also they derive satisfaction from 'the task'. Thus the leader combines task and socio-emotional leadership in himself.

Burke (1972) used laboratory groups and Bales IPA scoring system to compare task activities which had either **'high or low legitimacy'.** It was only in the latter that a clear separation of 'task' leadership and 'socio-emotional' leadership emerged.

(v) Leadership style

Contingency model of leadership effectiveness (Fiedler, 1964/67)

The effectiveness of the two styles of leadership was shown to be contingent on the favourability of the situation for the leader. Leaders were asked to evaluate on a number of scales their **'least preferred co-workers**

(LPC). It was assumed that if this LPC was given a high score, representing a favourable attitude, this was characteristic of a friendly, permissive and accepting style of leadership, whereas if there was a low LPC score this was typical of aloof, demanding, task orientated leaders.

The favourability of the situation was defined in terms of the ease the leader found in controlling and directing the members of the group. This was dependent in turn upon:

(i) **leader-member relations** : a favourable situation was one where the leader enjoyed the loyalty and confidence of the group

(ii) **task structure** : the more clearly structured the task the more favourable the situation

(iii) **the power of the leader** (defined in terms of the rewards and sanctions he had under his control) : the more powerful the leader the more favourable the situation.

Fiedler found that where the situation was either very favourable or very unfavourable the low LPC leaders were the most effective. On the other hand where the favourableness of the situation was intermediate then the high LPC leaders did better.

Criticisms of Fiedler

Fishbein et al (1969) suggest that the picture is blurred by the possibility that high and low LPC persons have a different kind of undesirable co-workers in mind when they make their judgements. The high LPC leader is irked by pushy, intelligent, dogmatic co-workers, while the low LPC leader is irritated by unfriendly, hostile, unpleasant and unwholesome characters.

Fiedler (1972) suggests that it only emerges in unfavourable circumstances whether a leader is employee or task-centred.

(vi) **Leadership and group climate**

Lewin, Lippit and White (1939) trained boys' club leaders to play three different types of leadership roles which they called autocratic, democratic and laissez-faire'.

(i) **The autocratic leader** gave orders, discouraged communication between the boys and was non-objective in his criticism and praise of the boys' work.

(ii) **The laissez-faire leader** opted out altogether and did not give orders or suggestions unless he was specifically asked.

(iii) **The democratic leader** helped the boys plan, made suggestions and listened to their suggestions, was concerned with their welfare and participated in the life of the group.

The leaders were well trained so that apart from the above, the performances were similar. They moved from club to club every six weeks changing their leadership style with each move. The boys in the groups were similar, ten year olds of similar intelligence, social background, etc. The behaviour patterns within the groups under different leaders were carefully recorded and conclusions drawn about the types of behaviour found under different styles of leadership.

Results

(i) **Autocratic leadership** : More work was achieved than under democratic leadership but group solidarity, originality and motivation to work were lower than in the democratic situation. Morale was lower and more aggressiveness and destructiveness was found.

(ii) **Democratic leadership** : While not so much work was done as in the 'autocratic' condition, morale was higher and the boys were more co-operative. They showed more approval of the leader and got more enjoyment out of the groups. Group solidarity, originality and initiative, and motivation to work were all higher.

(iii) **Laissez-faire leadership** : 'Not only was there less work done than in either of the other two conditions, but morale was low and behaviour disruptive as well.

Self assessment questions

1   What investigations have been made into the personality correlates of leadership? What conclusions (if any) can be drawn?

2   What conclusions have been drawn from studies of leadership functions?

3   What conclusions did Fiedler draw on the effect of leadership style on effectiveness?

4   What criticisms have been made of this?

5   Describe the study done by Lewin et al into leadership styles. What conclusions did they reach?

REFERENCES

Adorno T.W. et al 1950 The Authoritarian Personality New York Harper and Row.

Allport G. 1954 The Nature of Prejudice Reading Massachusetts Addison Wesley.

Asch S.E. 1952 Social Psychology New York Prentice Hall.

Asch S.E. 1956 Studies of independence and submission to group pressure. A minority of one against a unanimous majority in Psychological Monographs 70 (9).

Aronson E. and Mills J. 1959 The effect of severity of initiation on liking for a group. Journal of Abnormal and Social Psychology 59. 177-181.

Aronson E. 1969 "Some antecedents of interpersonal attraction" in W.J. Arnold and D. Levine (eds.) Nebraska Symposium on Motivation Lincoln University of Nebraska Press.

Bales R.F. 1950 Interaction Process Analysis: a method for the study of small groups. Cambridge Massachusetts Addison Wesley.

Bales R.F. 1970 Personality and Interpersonal Behaviour New York Holt Rinehart and Winston.

Bales R.F. and Slater P.E. 1955 Role differentiation in small decision-making groups in T. Parsons et al (eds). Family Socialization and Interaction Process New York Free Press.

Bandura A. 1973 Aggression: a social learning analysis. Englewood Cliffo Prentioe Hall.

Dandura A. 1977 Oocial Learning Theory Englewood Cliffs Prentice Hall.

Bandura A. and McDonald F.J. 1953 Influence of social reinforcement and behaviour of models on children's moral judgements. Journal of Abnormal and Social Psychology 47, 274-281.

Bandura A. and Walters R.H. 1963 Social Learning and Personality Development New York Holt Rinehart and Winston.

Baron R.A. 1978a Aggression and Heat "The long hot summer revisited" in A. Baum S. Valins and J. Singer (eds) Advances in Environmental Psychology Hillsdale New Jersey Lawrence Erlbaum Associates.

Baron R.A. 1978B The influence of hostile and non-hostile humour upon physical aggression. Bulletin of Personality and Social Psychology 4. 77-80.

Baron R.A. 1979 Heightened sexual arousal and physical aggression: an extension to females. Journal of Research in Personality 13. 91-102.

Baumrind D. 1964 Some thoughts on the ethics of research: after reading Milgram's study of obedience. American Psychologist 19. 421-3.

Bavelas A. 1950 Communication patterns in task oriented groups Journal of the Acoustical Society of America 2. 725-730.

Beaman A.L. Barnes P.J. Klentz B. and McQuirk B. 1978 Increasing helping rates through information dissemination: teaching pays: Personality and Social Psychology Bulletin 4. 406-411.

Bem D.J. 1972 Self perception theory in L. Berkowitz (ed.) Advances in Experimental Social Psychology Vol. 6 New York Academic Press.

Bem S.L. 1975 Fluffy women and chesty men in Psychology Today Sept. 1975.

Berkowitz L. Leyens J.P. West S.G. and Sebastian R.J. 1977 Some effects of violent and non-violent movies on behaviour of juvenile delinquents in L. Berkowitz (ed) Advances in Experimental Social Psychology Vol 10 New York Academic Press. p. 108.

Berkowitz L. 1978 "Whatever happened to the aggression frustration hypothesis?" American Behavioral Scientist 32. 691- 708.

Berscheid E. and Walster E. 1974 Physical Attractiveness in L. Berkowitz (ed) Advances in Experimental Social Psychology New York Academic Press.

Berscheid E. and Walster E. 1978 Interpersonal Attraction (2nd edition) Reading Massachusetts Addison Wesley.

Bogardus E.S. 1925 Measuring Social Distance Journal of Applied Sociology 9. 216-226.

Brehm W.J. and Cohen A. 1962 Explanation in Cognitive Dissonance. New York Wiley.

Brehm W.J. 1966 Theory of Psychological Reactance New York Academic Press.

Bruner J.S. Schapiro D. and Tagiuri R. The meaning of traits in isolation and in combination in R. Tagiuri and L. Petrullo (eds) Person Perception and Interpersonal Behaviour Stanford California Stanford University Press.

Bryan J.H. and Test M.A. 1967 Models and helping: naturalistic studies in aiding behaviour Journal of Personality and Social Psychology, 6. 400-

407.

Burke P.J. 1972 Leadership role differentiation in C.G. McClintock (ed) Experimenal Social Psychology New York Holt Rinehart and Winston.

Buss A.H. 1966A Instrumentality of aggression, feedback and frustration as determinants of physical aggression Journal of Personality and Social Psychology. 3. 153-162.

Byrne D. 1969 Attitudes and Attraction in L. Berkowitz (ed) Advances in Experimental Social Psychology Vol.4 New York Academic Press.

Byrne D. and Rhamey R. 1965 Magnitude of positive and negative reinforcements as a determinant of attraction. Journal of Personality and Social Psychology 2. 884-889.

Cartwright D. and Zander A. (eds) 1968 Group Dynamics: Research and Theory 3rd Edition New York Harper and Row.

Cattell R.B. and Nesselroade J.R. 1967 Likeness and completeness theories examined by the 16+ personality factor measure on stably and unstably married couples. Journal of Personality and Social Psychology 351-61.

Chaiken S. 1980 Heuristic versus systematic information processing and the use of source versus message cues in persuasion. Journal of Personality and Social Psychology 39. 752-766.

Cialdini R.B. Petty R.E. and Caccioppo J.T. 1981 Attitude and Attitude Change Annual Review of Psychology 32. 357-404.

Cialdini R.B. Levy A. Herman C.P. Koslowski L.T. and Petty R.E. 1976 Elastic shifts of opinion: determinants of direction and durability Journal of Personality and Social Psychology 34. 663-672.

Clark R.D. and Word L.E. 1972 Why don't bystanders help: because of ambiguity? Journal of Personality and Social Psychology 77. 221-229.

Collins B.G. and Hoyt M.G. 1972 Personal responsibility for consequences. An integration and extension of the forced compliance literature. Journal of Experimental Psychology 16. 199-206.

Collins B.E. and Raven B.H. 1969 Group structure: attraction coalitions communication and power in G. Lindzey and E. Aronson (eds) The Handbook of Social Psychology Vol.4 2nd edition Reading Massachusetts Addison Wesley.

Cooper J. and Croyle R.T. 1984 Attitudes and Attitude Change Annual Review of Psychology 35. 395-426.

Cottrell N.B. 1972 Social Facilitation in C.G. MacClintock (ed) Experimental Social Psychology New York Holt Rinehart and Winston.

Crutchfield R.S. 1954 A new technique for measuring individual differences in conformity to group judgement. Procedures of the Invitational Conference on Testing Problems pp. 69-74.

Dalshiell J.F. 1930 An experimental analysis of some group effects Journal of Personality and Social Psychology 25. 190- 199.

Darley J.M. and Latané B. 1970 Norms and normative behaviour: field studies of social interdependence in J. Macaulay and L. Berkowitz (eds) Altruism and Helping Behaviour New York Academic Press.

Dawkins R. 1978 The Selfish Gene Oxford University Press.

Dengerinck H.A. Schnedler R.W. and Covey M.V. 1978 The rule of avoidance in aggressive responses to attack and no attack Journal of Personality and Social Psychology 36. 1044-1053.

Deutsch M. and Krauss R.R. 1960 The effect of threat on interpersonal bargaining. Journal of Abnormal and Social Psychology 61. 181-189.

Diener E. 1979 Deindividuation: self awareness and disinhibition Journal of Personality and Social Psychology 37. 1160-1171.

Diener E. 1980 Deindividuation: the absence of self-awareness and self-regulation in group members in H.B. Paulus (ed) The Psychology of Group Influence Hillsdale New Jersey Erlbaum.

Dion K.K. Berscheid E. and Walster E. 1972 What is beautiful is good. Journal of Personality and Social Psychology 24. 285- 290.

Dollard J. Doob L.W. Miller N.E. Mowrer O.H. and Sears R.R. 1939. Frustration and Aggression New Haven Yale University Press.

Donnerstein E. and Wilson D.W. 1976 Effects of noise and perceived control on ongoing and subsequent aggressive behaviour. Journal of Personality and Social Psychology 36. 180-188.

Dorris J.W. 1972 Reactions to unconditional cooperation: a field study emphasising variables neglected in laboratory research. Journal of Personality and Psychology 22. 387-397.

Dyck R. and Rule B.G. 1978 The effect of causal attributions concerning attack on retribution. Journal of Personality and Social Psychology 36. 521-529.

Eron L.D. Huesmann L.R. Lefkowitz M.M. and Walder L.O. 1972 Does television violence cause aggression? American Psychologist 27. 253-262.

Eysenck H.J. 1953 Uses and Abuses of Psychology London Penguin.

Eysenck H.J. 1954 The Psychology of Politics London R.K.P.

Eysenck H.J. 1957 Sense and nonsense in Psychology London Penguin.

Eysenck H.J. 1982 Personality Genetics and Behaviour: Selected Papers New York Praeger.

Festinger L. 1957 A Theory of Cognitive Dissonance Evanston Illinois Row Peterson.

Festinger L. and Carlsmith J.J. 1959 Cognitive consequences of forced compliance. Journal of Abnormal and Social Psychology 58. 293-310.

Festinger L. Pepitone A. and Newcombe T.M. 1952 Some consequences of deinviduation in a group. Journal of Abnormal and Social Psychology 47. 383-398.

Festinger F.E. Schachter S. and Back K. 1950 Social Pressures in Informal Groups: a study of human factors in housing. New Yorker Harper and Row.

Fiedler F.E. 1964 A contingency model of leadership effectiveness in L. Berkowitz (ed) Advances in Experimental Social Psychology Vol.I New York Academic Press.

Fiedler F.E. 1967 A Theory of Leadership Effectiveness New York McGraw Hill.

Fishbein M. and Ajzen I. 1975 Attitude Intention and Behaviour: an introduction to theory and research. Reading Massachusetts Addison Wesley.

Fishbein M. Landy E. and Hatch G. 1969 Some determinants of an individual's esteem for his least preferred co-worker Human Relations 22. 172-288.

Fromkin H.L. Goldstein J.H. and Brock T.C. 1977 The role of "irrelevant" derogation in vicarious aggression catharsis: a field experiment Journal of Experimental Social Psychology 13.239-252.

Geen R.G. Stonner D. and Shope G.L. 1975 The facilitation of aggression: evidence against the catharsis hypothesis. Journal of Personality and Social Psychology 31. 721-726.

Gerbner G. and Gross L. 1976 The scary world of TV's heavy viewer Psychology Today 9. 41-45.

Gilbert G.M. 1951 Stereotype persistence and change among college students. Journal of Abnormal and Social Psychology 46. 245-254.

Gillig P.M. and Greenwald A.G. 1974 "Is it time to lay the sleeper effect to rest?" Journal of Personality and Social Psychology 29. 132-9.

Goldstein J.H. Davis R.W. and Herman D. 1975 Escalation of aggression: experimental studies. Journal of Perdonality and Social Psychology 31. 162-170.

Greenwell J. and Dengerinck H.A. 1973 The role of perceived versus actual attack in human physical aggression. Journal of Personality and Social Psychology 26. 66-71.

Harari H. and McDavid J.W. 1973 Name stereotypes and teacher's expectations. Journal of Educational Psychology 65. 222-225.

Harvey J. Harris B. and Barnes B. 1975 Actor observer differences in the perception of responsibility and freedom. Journal of Personality and Social Psychology 15. 158-164.

Heider F. 1958 The Psychology of Interpersonal Relations New York Wiley.

Hewitt J. 1972 Liking and the proportion of favourable evaluations. Journal of Personality and Social Psychology 22. 231-235.

Hill C.J. Rubin Z. and Peplan L.A. 1976 Breakups before marriage: the end of 103 affairs. Journal of Social Issues 32 (1). 147-68.

Hofling K.C. Brontzman E. Dalrymple S. Graves N. and Pierce C.M. 1966 An experimental study in the nurse physician relationship. Journal of Mental and Nervous Disorders 43. 171- 8.

Hokanson J.E. 1970 Psychophysiological evaluation of the catharsis hypothesis in K. Megargee and J.E. Hokanson (eds) The Dynamics of Aggression New York Harper and Row.

Hollander E.P. and Julian J.W. 1969 Contemporary trends in the analysis of the leadership processes. Psychological Bulletin 71. 387-97.

Horowitz E.L. 1936 Developing attitudes towards negroes in H. Proshansky and B. Scheidenberg (eds) Basic Studies in Social Psychology New York Holt Rinehart and Winston.

Hovland C.I. 1957 The order of presentation in persuasion. New Haven Connecticut Yale University Press.

Hovland C.I. and Mandell W. 1952 An experimental comparison of conclusion drawing by the communicator and the audience. Journal of Abnormal and Social Psychology 47. 581-8.

Hovland C.I. Lumsdaine A.A. and Sheffield F.D. 1949 Experiments in mass communication. Princeton Princeton University Press.

Hovland C.I. and Sherif M. 1952 Judgemental phenomena and scales of attitude measurement: item displacement in Thurstone scales. Journal of Abnormal and Social Psychology 47. 822-832.

Hovland C.I. and Weiss W. 1951 The influence of source credibility on communication effectiveness. Public Opinion Quarterly 151. 635-50.

Hunt P.J. and Hillery J.M. 1973 Social facilitation at different stages in learning. Paper presented to the Mid-Western Psychological Association Meetings Cleveland Ohio.

Izard C.E. 1960 Personality similarity and friendship. Journal of Abnormal and Social Psychology 61. 45-51.

Jacklin C.N. and Maccoby E.E. 1978 Social behaviour at 33 months in same sex and mixed sex dyads. Child Development 49. 557-569.

Jacobs P.A. Brunton M. and Melville M.M. 1965 Aggressive behaviour, mental abnormality and the XXY male. Nature 208. 1351-1352.

Janis I.L. and Feshback S. 1963 The effects of fear arousing communications. Journal of Abnormal and Social Psychology 48. 78-92.

Jones E.E. Davis K.E. and Gergen K.J. 1961 Role playing variations and their informational value for person perception. Journal of Abnormal and Social Psychology 63. 302-310.

Jones E.E. and Davis K.E. 1965 From acts to disposition: the attribution process in person perception in L. Berkowitz (ed) Advances in Experimental Social Psychology New York Academic Press.

Karlins M. Coffman T.L. and Walters G. 1969 "On the fading of social stereotypes: studies in three generations of college students". Journal of Personality and Social Psychology 13. 1- 16.

Katz D. and Braly K. 1933 Racial stereotypes of 100 college students Journal of Abnormal and Social Psychology 28. 280-90.

Katz D. Glucksberg S. and Krauss R. 1960 Needs satisfaction and Edwards PPS scores in married couples Journal of Cons. Psychology 24. 305-8.

Kelly H.H. 1967 Attribution Theory in Social Psychology in D. Levine (eds) Nebraska Symposium on Motivation 15. 142-238.

Kelly G.A. 1955 The Psychology of Personal Constructs New York Norton.

Kelman H.C. 1953 Attitude change as a function of response restriction Human Relations 6. 185-214.

Kelman H.C. and Hovland C.I. 1953 Reinstatement of the communicator in delayed measurement of opinion change Journal of Abnormal and Social Psychology 48 327-335.

Kilham W. and Mann L. 1974 Level of destructive obedience as a function of transmitter and executant roles in Milgram's obedience paradigm, Journal of Personality and Social Psychology 29 696-702.

Kimble C.E. Fitz D. and Onorad J. The effectiveness of counter aggression strategies in reducing interactive aggression by males Journal of Personality and Social Psychology 35 272- 278.

Krebs D. and Adinolfs A.A. 1975 Physical attractiveness, social relations and personality style. Journal of Personality and Social Psychology 31 245-253.

Kretch D Crutchfield R.A. and Ballachey E.L. 1962 Individual in Society: a textbook of Social Psychology New York McGraw Hill.

Laljee M. Watson M. and White P. 1982 Explanations attributions and the social context of unexpected behaviour European Journal of Social Psychology 12 (1) 17-29.

Latané B. and Darley J.M. 1968 Group inhibition of bystander intervention in emergencies Journal of Personality and Social Psychology 10 215-221.

Latané B. and Darley J.M. 1970 The unresponsive bystander: why doesn't he help? New York Appleton-Century- Crofts.

Leavitt H.J. 1951 Some effects of certain communication patterns on group performance Journal of Abnormal and Social Psychology 46 38-50.

Lebon G. 1895 The Crowd London Ernest Benn.

Lerner M.J. and Lichtman R.R. 1968 Effects of perceived norms on attitudes and altruistic behaviour towards a dependent other Journal of Personality and Social Psychology 9 226-232.

Leventhal H.R. Singer P. and Jones S. 1965 Effects of fear and specificity of recommendation upon attitudes and behaviour Journal of Personality and Social Psychology 2 20- 29.

Lewin K. Lippitt R. and White R.K. 1939 Patterns of aggressive behaviour in experimentally created social climates Journal of Social Psychology 10 271-279.

Likert R. 1932 A technique for measuring attitudes Archives of Psychology 2 1-55.

Loew C.A. 1967 Acquisition of a hostile attitude and its relationship to aggressive behaviour Journal of Personality and Social Psychology 5 335-341.

Luce R.D. and Raiffa H. 1957 Games and Decisions New York Wiley.

McArthur L.A. 1972 The how and the what of why: some determinants and consequences of causal attribution Journal of Personality and Social Psychology 22 171-193.

McArthur L. and Post D. 1977 Figural emphasis and person perception Journal of Experimental Social Psychology 13 520- 536.

McClintock C.G. and McNeel S.P. 1966 Reward level and game playing behaviour Journal of Conflict Resolution 10 98- 102.

McGrath J.E. and Altman I. 1966 Small Group Research New York Holt Rinehart and Winston.

McGuire W.J. 1969 The nature of attitudes and attitude change in Lindzey G. and Aronson E. (eds) Handbook of Social Psychology 2nd edition Vol 3 Reading Massachusetts Addison Wesley.

McGuire W.J. 1968 Personality and susceptibility to social influence in E. Borgatta and W. Lambert (eds) Handbook of Personality Theory and Research Vol 3 Chicago Rand McNally.

Malkis F.S. Kalle R.J. and Tedeschi J.T. 1982 Attitudinal politics in the forced compliance situation Journal of Social Psychology 117 79-91.

Mann L. 1969 Social Psychology New York Wiley

Mantell D.M. 1971 The potential for violence in Germany Journal of Social Issues 27(4) 101-112.

Markus H. 1978 Self schemata and processing information about self Journal of Personality and Social Psychology 35 63-78.

Maslow C. Yoselson K. and London M. 1971 Persuasiveness of confidence expressed via language and body language British Journal of Social and Clinical Psychology 10 234-240.

Michener J. Kent State: what happened and why New York Random House.

Milgram S. 1963 Behavioural study of obedience Journal of Abnormal and Social Psychology 67 371-378.

Miller N. Maryuama G. Beaber R.J. and Valone K. Speed of speech and persuasion Journal of Personality and Social Psychology 34 615-624.

Mueller C. and Donnerstein E. 1977 The effects of humour induced arousal on aggressive behaviour Journal of Research in Personality 11 73-82.

Mulder M. 1960 Communication Structure Decision Structure and Group Performance Sociometry 23 1-14.

Newcombe T.M. 1961 The acquaintance process New York Holt Rinehart and Winston.

Nisbett R.E. and Ross L. 1980 Human Inferences: strategies and shortcomings of social judgement Englewood Cliffs New Jersey Prentice Hall.

Orne M.T. 1962 On the social psychology of the psychological experiment - with particular reference to demand characteristics and their implications in Americal Psychologist 17 (11) 776-783.

Osgood C.E. Suci G.J. and Tannenbaum P.H. 1957 The measurement of meaning Urbana Illinois University of Illinois Pres.

Pettigrew T.F. 1958 Personality and cultural factors in inter-group attitudes: a cross national comparison: in Journal of Conflict Resolution 2 29-42.

Petty R.E. and Caccioppo J.T. 1979 Effects of forewarning of persuasive interest and involvement on cognitive responses and persuasion Personality and Social Psychology Bulletin 5 173- 176.

Petty R.E. and Caccioppo J.T. 1981 Attitudes and Persuasion: classic and contemporary approaches Dubuque Iowa Wm. C. Brown.

Pushkin I. 1967 A study of ethnic choice in the play of young children in three London districts Unpublished doctoral thesis University of London.

Rabbie J.M. and Horowitz M. 1960 Arousal of in-group, out-group bias by a chance minor loss Journal of Personality and Social Psychology 13 237-266.

Rapport A. and Chammah A. 1965 The Prisoner's Dilemma Ann Arbor University of Michigan Press.

Rokeach M. 1960 The Open and Closed Mind New York Basic Books.

Rosenberg M.J. and Hovland C.I. 1960 Cognitive, affective and behaviour components of attitudes in Hovland C.I. and Rosenberg M.J. (eds) Attitude Organisation and Change: an analysis of consistency among attitude components New Haven Connecticut Yale University Press.

Rosenberg S. and Jones R.A. 1972 A method for investigating and representing a person's implicit theory of personality: Theodore Dreissen's view of people Journal of Personality and Social Psychology 20 372-386.

Ross L. Amabile T. Steinmetz J. 1977 Social Rules, Social Control and Biases in Social Perception Processes Journal of Personality and Social Psychology 35 485-494.

Ross A.S. and Braband J. 1973 The effect of increased responsibility on bystander intervention II: the cue value of a blind person Journal of Personality and Social Psychology 25 254-258.

Saegert S. Swap W. and Zajonc R.B. 1973 Eposure context and interpersonal attraction Journal of Personality and Social Psychology 25 234-242.

Schneider D.J. Hastorf A.H. and Ellsworth P.C. 1979 Person Perception 2nd edition Reading Massachusetts Addison Wesley.

Secord P.F. and Backman C.W. 1974 Social Psychology New York McGraw Hill.

Shanab M.E. and Kahya K.A. 1977 A behavioural study of obedience in children Journal of Personality and Social Psychology 35 530-536.

Shaw M.E. 1954 Some effects of problem complexity upon problem solution efficiency in different communication nets Journal of Experimental Psychology 48 211-217.

Sherif M. 1935 A study of some social factors in perception Archives of Psychology 27 No. 187.

Sherif M. 1951 Experimental study of intergroup relations in Rohwer J.H. and Sherif M. (eds) Social Psychology at the Crossroads New York Harper and Row.

Sherif M. and Hovland C.I. 1961 Social Judgement: assimilation and contrast in communication and attitude change New Haven Connecticut Yale University Press.

Sherif M. Sherif C.W. and Nebergall R.C. 1965 Attitudes and attitude change: the social judgement involvement approach Philadelphia Saunders.

Sherif M. et al 1961 Intergroup conflict and cooperation - The Robber's Cave Experiment Norman Institute of Group Relations University of Oklahoma.

Smith M.B. Bruner J.S. and White R.W. 1956 Opinions and Personality New York Wiley.

Star S.A. Williams R.M. and Struffer S.A. 1958 Negro infantry platoons in white companies in Maccoby E Newcombe T.M. and Hartley E (eds) Readings in Social Psychology 3rd edition New York Holt Rinehart and Winston.

Taylor S. Fiske S. Close M. Anderson C. and Ruderman A. 1979 Solo status as a psychological variable: the power of being distinctive Unpublished manuscript Harvard University Press.

Taylor S.P. Gammon C.B. and Capasso D.R. 1976 Aggression as a function of the interaction of alcohol and threat Journal of Personality and Social Psychology 34 938-941.

Tedeschi J.T. 1981 Impression Management Theory and Social Psychological Research New York Academic Press.

Tedeschi J.T. Schlenken B.R. and Bonoma T.V. 1971 Cognitive Dissonance: a private ratiocination or public spectacle American Psychologist 26 685-695.

Thibault J.W. and Kelley H.H. 1978 Interpersonal: a theory of interdependence New York Wiley.

Thomas A. Chess S. and Birch H.G. 1970 The Origin of Personality Scientific American 223(2) 102-109.

Thurstone L.L. and Chase E.J. 1929 Measurement of Attitudes Chicago University of Chicago Press.

Triandis H.C. 1971 Attitudes and Attitude Change New York Wiley.

Triplett N. 1898 Dynamogenic factors in pacemaking and competion American Journal of Psychology 9 507-533.

Verba S. 1961 Small Groups and Political Behviour Princeton Princeton University Press.

Voissem N.H. and Sistrunk F. 1971 Communication schedule and cooperative game behaviour Journal of Personality and Social Psychology 19 160-167.

Walster E. and Festinger L. 1962 The effectiveness of overhead persuasive communications Journal of Abnormal and Social Psychology 61 159-167

Weatherly D. 1964 Anti semitism and the expression of fantasy aggression Journal of Abnormal and Social Psychology 62 454- 457.

West S.G. and Wicklund R.H. 1980 A Primer of Social Psychological Theories Monterey Brooks/Cole.

Wheeler L. 1966 Toward a Theory of Behavioural Contagion Psychological Review 75 179-92.

Winch R.F. Ktanes T. and Ktanes V. 1954 Theory of complementary needs in mate selection: an analytic and descriptive study American Sociological Review 29 241-9.

Witkin H.A. et al 1976 Criminality in XYY and XXY Men Science 1976 196: 547-555.

Zajonc R.B. 1965 Social Facilitation Science 149: 269- 274.

Zajonc R.B. 1980 Thinking and feeling: preferences need no inferences American Psychologist 35 151-157.

Zajonc R.B. Heingartner A. and Herman E.M. 1969 Social enhancement and impairment of performance in the cockroach Journal of Personality and Social Psychology 13 83-92.

Zanna M.P. and Cooper J. 1974 Dissonance and the pill: an attribution approach to studying the arousal properties of dissonance Journal of Personality and Social Psychology 29 703-709.

Zanna M.P. Kiesler C.A. and Pilkonis P.A. 1970 Positive and negative attitudinal affect established by classical conditioning Journal of Personality and Social Psychology 14 321-328.

Zillman D. 1979 Hostility and Aggression Hillside New Jersey Erlbaum Associates.

Zimbardo P.G. 1960 Involvement and communication discrepancy as determinants of opinion conformity Journal of Abnormal and Social Psychology 60 86-94.

Zimbardo P.G. 1970 The Human Choice: individuation reason and order versus deindividuation impulse and chaos in W.J. Arnold and D. Levine (eds) Nebraska Symposium on Motivation 1969 Vol 16 Lincoln University of Nebraska Press.

Zimbardo P.G. Banks W.C. Craig H. and Jaffe D. 1973 A pirandellian prison: the mind is a formidable jailor New York Times Magazine April 8th 1973 38-60.

INDEX